"A very touching story that poign[a] have discovered 'the truth,' the s[p] have been led to believe."

— *New Age Journal*

"This is a book for anyone who wants to heal themselves, heal others or understand the nature of the mind-body connection. Sheri Perl has created a masterpiece which brings hope, inspiration and life changing tools in the Sheri Perl Healing Program outlined in Chapter nine. Yet for all its profound wisdom it is easy to read, written with humility, honesty and vulnerability.

We seriously wish that it could be set as required reading for any aspiring healer so that they can really grasp Harry Edwards understanding that "when healing energy is directed to the dis-ease that is underlying the disease, the potential exists to cure anything, even diseases considered medically incurable."

— Victor Zammit LLB. PhD. and Wendy Zammit M.A. Co-authors of *A Lawyer Presents the Evidence for the Afterlife* and *The Friday Afterlife Report*

I could not stop reading this profoundly simple account of personal transformation and healing. An inspiration!"

— Barbara Marx Hubbard, Co-founder, Global Family

"An extraordinarily personal testament of experiencing the basic alchemy of creation."

— Hazel Henderson, Author of, *The Politics of the Solar Age*

"It is rare that one person's true story can be compelling, instructive, and entertaining in equal measures. Healing from the Inside Out is all that. Sheri offers up her personal healing journey in a highly relate-able way that is sure to touch hearts."

— Susanne Wilson, Author & Spiritual Teacher

"Sheri Perl's story of her amazing healing, after enduring years of illness that few could have survived, is a story of hope for all of us. In unexpected and unusual ways, she was miraculously healed and has devoted the rest of her life to helping others physically, emotionally and spiritually. Hers is one of the most encouraging and helpful stories you will ever read or hear, and gives hope to all of us, that there is an unseen dimension and spiritual help beyond anything most of us could ever imagine. Great story - great book!"

— Anne Puryear, author of *Stephen Lives!* My Son Stephen, his life, suicide and afterlife.

HEALING

from the

INSIDE OUT

and the

OUTSIDE IN

by
Sheri Perl

For more information about the author Sheri Perl
visit her website:

www.sheriperl.com.

There you will also find information about *The Prayer Registry*, Sheri's free prayer service for bereaved parents and their children-in-spirit.

Sheri Perl and Harry Edwards 1972

This book is dedicated to the late spiritual healer,

Harry Edwards, my healer.

Harry's gift of healing brought health to my body

and introduced me to the reality of spirit.

His presence in my life

turned my life around and

opened the doors to an exploration

of spirit that continues today.

I owe him more than I can say.

Introduction

As I look back at my past, it is hard for me to believe that I, as such a young woman, could have suffered and triumphed over so much pain and illness. As a mother of three I can't imagine how I could ever endure watching my children suffer as my mother stood by and watched me. And yet sitting here now, I have no regrets. I know that in a very real way, I am better, stronger, wiser, and more compassionate as a result of what I have been through.

My illnesses changed the direction of my life dramatically by propelling me into spirituality as a path to healing when medical science could do no more. I was a young woman of only 20 years when the spiritual healing that you will read about in the following pages took place. No one could have been more surprised at the positive outcome than I, who was a total non-believer at the time, with no prior exposure to spirituality.

The first part of this book is a memoir that tells my story which has been in print since 1989 under the title "Healing From the Inside Out." It walks the reader through my experience with illness, western medicine and spiritual healing. Nothing in that story has changed. The second part of this book, however, is all new material because between 1971 and the present, my ideas have changed. In fact, as you will see, over the course of time, my views swung from one end of the spectrum to the other leaving no middle ground.

I started out believing that healing the body was only achieved through western medicine, or from the outside-in. After my life-changing healing experience I believed that healing could only come through spirit, or from the inside-out.

I

After living another four decades I have come to see that there is great wisdom in walking what I call the middle road. When you walk the middle road, you are not compelled to make a choice between the spiritual and the physical. Instead you are free to use anything that will help you.

After all I have seen, I am fond of saying, "Keep an open mind because you never know where the healing will come from." Sometimes something as simple as what you put into your mouth makes a critical difference in your health. As I see it now, healing involves what you do from the outside-in every bit as much as what you do from the inside out. They work best when they work together.

It is my hope that this book will open your eyes to the realm of spirit that dwells within this very world of which we are a part. I wish this for you because I have found that when you incorporate spirit into your life the benefits are palpable. I know to some of you, this may sound unfathomable, but hear me out. At the very least, I believe that my story will peak your curiosity.

It is my intention, however, to leave you with more than a story. The remainder of this book is devoted to sharing the techniques and the wisdom that has helped me to survive and move forward at the most difficult times of my life. In gratitude I want to share all that I can with you in the hope that my experience will serve as a torchlight to help illuminate your path.

SHERI PERL
February 19, 2016

Table of Contents

Chapter One

My First Illness

In the summer of 1967, I was touring the West Coast with a group of thirty girls when the first symptoms of illness appeared. The daughter of a wealthy businessman, I was a healthy, attractive, normal sixteen-year-old girl. I was in no way prepared for the events that were about to take place in my life.

The teen tour had started off on a high note. I had become close with eleven other girls and we instantly formed a clique. We called ourselves "the dirty dozen," passed around pictures of our boyfriends, compared and tried on each other's clothing, and engaged in the normal conversations of young women. There was nothing that could have prepared me for the severe pain that seemed to come upon me from out of nowhere one morning while we were visiting the Grand Canyon. While all the other girls were getting dressed to go down to breakfast, I found that I was unable to get out of my bed. "I must have eaten something," I thought, "this will pass soon." I had never experienced serious illness before. Naturally, I assumed that the sharp abdominal pain would go away as mysteriously as it came.

I informed my mother of the difficulty I was having two days after it began. The sympathy in her voice made me feel like bursting into tears, and yet I fought hard to hold my emotions inside. I wanted so to be grown up. Determined not to appear the baby, I refused my mother's requests to return home, visiting more bathrooms in Disneyland than exhibits.

The rest of the tour was a nightmare. From the time the symptoms began until our arrival back in Kennedy Airport eight weeks later, there was not one day in which I wasn't plagued with severe discomfort. I became increasingly crankier and more preoccupied as my illness progressed. As a result, the other girls, who considered themselves very worldly and sophisticated, grew impatient. I felt very shut off from them, even disliked. I ached with loneliness.

During the tour I grew used to the condition, which somehow made it more bearable. I could pretty much expect to have cramps periodically throughout the day and an intense case of the runs every morning. But frighteningly, a new symptom developed the last ten days of the trip which was more acute and disturbing. I began to experience pain in my esophagus whenever I swallowed. Simultaneously, I felt an itch behind my right ear. I knew that I wasn't going crazy, but all of this was very unnerving. Because the other girls seemed so annoyed with my complaints, I was afraid to open up to them. Therefore, I held my fear inside of myself, along with the hope that when I returned home, I would see a good doctor capable of curing me.

I could clearly see the concern on both my parents' faces when we finally met again at Kennedy Airport. They, too, had expected my condition to clear up by now, and they were anxious for me to start medical treatment. My mother watched me in amazement as I cried and kissed each girl good-bye, promising to write and pretending a kinship I didn't feel. She knew that I felt estranged from the girls, and was surprised to see the measures I would take to pretend otherwise. I was a little surprised myself, but while I remained in the company of others, I felt the pressure to fit in. I was relieved now to be separate from the girls and the traveling. No longer would I have to contend with filthy train bathrooms or the impatient looks of annoyance from the other girls. The sight of my father in the front seat, dark and handsome, like a sheik, and my mother, blond and fair-skinned, like an angel, created a feeling of security. I couldn't remember a time in my entire sixteen years when a problem arose that they could not solve. Yet a sense of foreboding pervaded the air as we drove to suburban New Jersey.

My parents were determined that I see a doctor immediately. Of course, I knew that this was inevitable, and I feared it greatly. I presume that most people don't particularly enjoy going to the doctor, but to me it had always been an enormous trauma. I received more than one polio shot on the sidewalk outside my doctor's office, when the nurse had finally put a stop to my getaway. I found taking my clothes off and sitting on the white paper uncomfortable and embarrassing. The very thought of needles scared the hell out of me. It is a good thing that I had no idea of what lay ahead.

As the car pulled into the circular driveway that led to our home, I felt as if I had never left. Everything looked just as it had before, green and lush and beautiful. My brothers Rich and Rob were home to greet me, along with "Dee" - Louise Miller, our live-in governess. She had joined the family at Richard's birth in 1957. Our cook Mamie, who made the best southern fried chicken in the world (as far as we were concerned) had prepared her specialty in honor of my return. Everything was just as it had been, except for one thing. I was unable to eat my chicken dinner without experiencing the familiar pain in my abdomen, and the unfamiliar pain and itch combo in my esophagus and ear.

An internist, a friend of my father's, was the first doctor to see me. He had been treating my father for high blood pressure for a few years, and my parents thought that he might be able to help me. At least they knew him. Surely it would be a good place to start.

On the day of our appointment I was as nervous as a jackrabbit. I thoroughly resented the experience from start to finish. My mother and I sat nervously together in the waiting room for quite some time until a nurse took my personal history and then led me to a room where I was instructed to undress and put on one of those obscene paper gowns. I was then asked to trot off to the bathroom and provide a little urine sample, and then to come back and sit on the table and wait for the doctor--how I hated that white paper! When the doctor entered the room, I was glad that he was a small man and not very intimidating. Nonetheless my stomach seemed to turn over a few times as he examined me, drew blood from my arm, and then ran some X rays of my esophagus. Due to my obsession with the esophagus problem, I completely glossed over the abdominal pain in my discussion with the doctor, which led him to diagnose and treat only the esophagus situation. He said my esophagus looked a little swollen in one place, that it was probably a result of nerves, and he prescribed a muscle relaxer to be taken a half hour before meals. He said that it would probably improve within a week or two and that he didn't find anything else wrong with me.

My mother and I left. As I look back I realize that this day marked the beginning of our medical companionship. As we drove to the pharmacy to fill the prescription, I was satisfied. The dreaded doctor's appointment was over and I was free again to live my life. My mother, on the other hand, expressed her dismay over the fact that no light had been shed on my digestive problems. She wanted me to see another doctor, while I just wanted to be left alone. I had accepted the stomach problem. I didn't want to see it get in the way of my enjoyment any more than it already had. My boyfriend was about to leave for his freshman year in college, and we wanted to attend a number of social events. I was anticipating an eventful and exciting junior year as a member of the Millburn High School cheer leading squad, a status that I had worked very hard to achieve. I didn't have time to be sick. Moreover, I had grown so used to the symptoms that I figured the best action was to take no action at all. Of course, my reasoning was powered by my fear of doctors. My parents were aware of this, and were not going to go along with it. They had enormous faith in the medical profession and felt that once we found the right doctor, my problems would be over. The decision was handed down to me by my father while he sat in his chair at the head of the long dining-room table: I'd see another doctor and we would not give up until I was completely well again. It was inconceivable and ludicrous to my parents that this should not come about. They could not accept the notion that I would just continue to live with pain and discomfort. My father's presence was always very strong and I knew that I could not buck him. An appointment was made.

The next man who treated me was a gastroenterologist, a specialist in digestive disorders. Dr. Marvin, with whom I would eventually have a long and involved relationship, seemed very alien and distant to me as he first walked into the examining room. There I was, biting my nails, wearing one of those daring little examining robes, sitting on the white paper. My mother stood just a few feet away from me. I sensed a ripple of fear shoot through both of us as our hope walked in the door.

The doctor was not very cheerful or communicative as he went about his business of listening to my heart, taking my blood pressure, and pressing on my stomach to see where it hurt. My mother held my hand as the doctor drew blood from my other arm. No one knew better than she how terrified I'd always been of needles. Holding hands became a ritual with us, symbolizing to me that we were both in this together. The doctor then asked me to drink two large glasses of a pink chalky liquid and explained to me how the barium would illuminate my intestinal tract, thus allowing him to have a closer look inside. As I lay on the cold X-ray table with a cup in my hand and a straw in my mouth, Dr. Marvin, from inside a booth, would say, "Now take a drink, drink, drink, now hold it, hold your breath, hold it, okay, breathe."

My mother and I couldn't believe it when the doctor reported that the X rays showed nothing conclusive. There was no diagnosis to be made and no treatment to be instituted. He recommended trying antacids but no further instructions were given.

My mother was thoroughly disheartened. I was so glad to get my ass off the white paper and onto the seat of the car that all I could experience was enormous relief. As we drove home, I resolved to sweep the symptoms under the rug whenever I could. My plan was to find a way to just live around them.

I continued this way throughout the rest of the summer of 1967 and into the fall. We were now approaching 1968, a new year. I was moving toward it with a condition that was bearable, yet constant. I made certain adjustments in order to deal with my symptoms. For example, by this time I had developed such a bad case of hemorrhoids that immediately after stepping out of bed in the morning, I would start running a bath. This way I could dive into the warm soothing water as soon as my angry bowels granted me parole from the toilet. Beyond such small adjustments, I tried to maintain what I considered to be a normal existence, attending school and interacting socially. As a teen I did not understand my fear or my motivations. I constantly pushed myself to keep active, and cover up my illness rather than address it.

My home life was bustling and active. My younger brothers, ten-year-old Richie and eight-year-old Bobby, were not fully aware of my illness. My parents didn't believe in telling children upsetting things. For the most part I behaved normally, and an occasional whine was not seen as anything out of the ordinary. Sondra, my oldest sister by four years, was a junior at Simmons College in Boston and was not overly alarmed about my health either. My siblings and I had never experienced any serious illness, and we naturally did not anticipate one now.

As for my parents, they had been through transitions and changes all of their lives, and outside of this growing concern that they felt for me, their lives were blossoming. My father was achieving financial security, very important to the son of struggling immigrant parents. Through skill and tenacity he had developed a thriving business with many employees. He was proud to provide for his family as his own parents had been unable to provide for him. We moved from impoverished Newark to patrician Short Hills. By the time I was ten years old, I was living in the lap of luxury. I had my own room, with my own private bathroom, equipped with both a tub and shower stall. My room was large, all decorated in my favorite color, pink, complete with a luscious pink canopy bed. We lived in a truly fantastic house with a basement large enough for many parties and an indoor swimming pool, which kept us busy after school and on weekends.

Our life in Short Hills sounds elegant, I know, but for me (and Sondra as well), it required difficult adjustments. We had lived our early life in predominantly Jewish neighborhoods. I took for granted the fact that I always fit in. In the Short Hills school system, however, I was the only Jewish girl in the two fourth-grade classes, and for the first time in my life I was exposed to anti-Semitism. A number of the children said that they could not play with me because I killed their God. It made no sense to me, but I was nonetheless hurt by it. The years in Short Hills were not easy, happy, or carefree ones for me or Sondra, who had similar experiences with her classmates.

But for my father, the house was wonderful, a symbol of the security and life-style he never had. Everything in his adult life was flowing just as he wanted it to, and he felt powerful and in control. I knew this, and that my mother shared his happiness. I wanted to do nothing to endanger it.

As winter turned to spring, however, I found it more difficult to cover up my illness. My symptoms became more frequent and severe. I began to double over from pain that deeply laced into me and did not pass so quickly. My parents were alarmed. My mother made an appointment with Dr. Marvin right away.

I remember the day prior to my appointment quite clearly. Toward the afternoon my mother nervously explained to me that I could not partake in the family barbecue as I was allowed only a liquid supper, with no food or water at all after twelve midnight. To make matters worse, before I went to bed I had to take two tablespoons of Castor Oil. I obeyed reluctantly, not anticipating that in two hours I would wake to spend the rest of the night running to the bathroom. In the morning I was tired and drained. I was shocked when my mother came into my room, this time carrying an enema, which she said I would have to use, doctor's orders. We argued back and forth as I sought desperately for a way out. "Your bowels have to be completely empty," she explained, "or the X rays cannot be done." "Completely empty? Completely empty!" I wailed. "What do you think they are now, full?" I eventually surrendered. Upset and exhausted, we both arrived at the doctor's office.

My father accompanied us. He knew how difficult I could be about doctors, and how painful it would be for my mother to handle me alone. She would need his support, and I his firm hand.

At the office the sight of a tray full of long silver tubes sent waves of panic throughout my system. When I asked the nurse what they were for, she replied that they were for the doctor to look into my rectum. I took one more look at those tubes, thought about the idea of the doctor putting them into me, and ran. "Over my dead body," I yelled as I dashed in a panic to find my parents. Of course I was soon back in the examination room.

Dr. Marvin requested that I try to be mature as he rotated the table I was leaning over so that my head was down and my bare bottom was up in the air. I screamed as I felt the cold metal tube pressing its way into my body, shocked at my pain and humiliation. When it was over, I again ran to my parents and begged them to take me home now! But there was still more testing to do.

This time I was positioned on one of the X-ray tables in the back of the office. I expected to be given a glass of chalky barium and was shocked when I saw the nurse attach an enema bag to a pole close to the table. The next thing I knew the nurse was trying to put the tube into me. I practically flew off the table and ran into the waiting room. Again the same scene ensued and I ended up back on the X-ray table with the tube inside me. I felt small, embarrassed, humiliated. For my bowels, which had been ill for almost a year now, the barium enema was irritating and painful. What a relief it was when I could at last empty my bowels of all the barium that had been shot into them. It was an even greater relief when I was told that the tests were done and I could dress.

At this point my father left my mother and me to meet with the doctor and hear his report. My mother looked nervous and worn as we waited. We felt impatient and anxious to hear what he had to say.

"Mrs. Perl," he said, "your daughter has ileitis, a disease of the small intestine, also known as Crohn's disease or regional enteritis. It is a chronic disease and we have no cure for it."

No cure? My mother looked crestfallen. "Are you saying, doctor, that there is nothing that you can do?" asked my mother. Dr. Marvin said, "We have some drugs that have been helpful in controlling the growth of the disease, but at this point in time we cannot cure it, although researchers are working diligently to discover a cure."

Somehow the reality of what he was saying couldn't sink in. "I just don't understand," my mother said, "surely there's got to be some way for my daughter to recover."

"In some cases," Dr. Marvin continued, "the disease goes into remission, and the patient can feel wonderful." Remission. We liked the sound of that. It was the only positive word we had heard yet.

"What does that mean?" my mother probed further. "Does it mean that Sheri can be well again?" A thread of hope, a crust of bread, we'd take anything!

"Not exactly," said the doctor. "Remission is a period in which the patient feels well but, in actuality, the disease still exists as it is not curable." It all sounded like a bunch of mumbo-jumbo to us. How could it be possible for this illness to just go on and on indefinitely? The doctor went on to say that in extreme cases surgery was an option, but was certainly not something that we should consider at this time.

Dr. Marvin placed me on a bland diet, eliminating fresh fruit, fresh vegetables, roughage of any kind, milk and all milk products, spices or condiments, and all fried foods. I was a picky eater to begin with; now it would be even harder for my mother to put together meals that would appeal to me. He also started me on drug therapy, beginning first with sulfa drugs in an attempt to control the spread of the disease, and codeine pills to help with the pain. By the time I returned to school, in early spring, I had a number of different pill bottles with instructions for taking some before meals, others after meals, some in the A.M. and some in the P.M. I didn't take any of it too seriously, relying upon my mother to keep it all straight. Dr. Marvin also insisted that we make an appointment with an associate of his in Manhattan, a man well known for his work with this disease. He felt it was essential that we confirm his diagnosis and treatment with another opinion. And so an appointment was made.

I didn't like this doctor very much, He seemed cool, abrupt, and unsympathetic. He checked out my X rays, insisted on doing his own rectal examination (which of course caused another mini-ordeal for me), and then announced that he concurred with the diagnosis of Crohn's disease, as well as the present course of treatment. All he had to add was his opinion that I rest more, probably even give up my position as cheerleader, and accept the fact that I was a very sick girl. Ugh!

I found myself drifting further and further away from my high-school friends and into myself. It seemed that they had no idea of what my life was like anymore and, by contrast, their interests seemed trivial and superficial to me. Instead I developed my relationship with Steve, my boyfriend. He was in his freshman year at Colgate University in Hamilton, New York, and most nights would find me buried in my father's den where I was able to make use of a long-distance watts line, whiling the hours away. Talking to Steve gave me something to look forward to. I could pour my heart out to him, sharing the most intimate details of my illness, and he never seemed to mind or grow impatient. He always had a humorous way of looking at the situation, as well as something warm and comforting to say. Our conversations became the highlight of my life.

It was around this time that my sister became involved with a handsome young surgical intern. Barry Mankowitz possessed many attractive qualities. He was a sweet man, handsome and intelligent. He was also responsible, and incredibly clean-cut, and in 1968 those qualities were becoming a rarity. Barry not only impressed my sister but my parents as well.

He proposed marriage to Sondra six short weeks after he met her. She accepted, although she was confused about her feelings toward him. I always wonder about the forces that brought them together because of the enormous role Barry would play in saving my life.

By the fall of my senior year I found it impossible to maintain my activities as a cheerleader. At the first few football games of the season, I tried to get by, mouthing the words to the cheers, feeling too tired to jump and shout at the same time. Soon it became apparent that the jumping alone was too much for me. It was a sad day for me when I handed over my uniform and megaphone to an excited classmate. As my mother pulled into the school driveway to take me home (I was too upset to remain in school that day), I began to ask if it mattered anyway. I wondered how something as trivial as cheerleading could matter if one could get so sick. "Who cared?" I rationalized. I did!

By this time I was thinner, weaker, and living with even greater pain. Dr. Marvin had tried a number of sulfa drugs, but none helped. The only pills that seemed to work were the pain killers, which I soon came to see relieved anxiety as well as pain. Unfortunately, even they were being rendered impotent by this monster that was growing in strength and power with each passing day.

It was Sondra who had the courage to speak honestly with me then. She and I had always been close and now, with Barry her fiancée, she knew more facts about my illness than I. I was surprised to learn from her that Barry thought my illness was very serious, more serious than I wanted to believe. I wanted to believe that things couldn't get any worse. But then it happened.

It was all planned and meant to be a beautiful fun-filled weekend. Steve and I, leaving from Colgate, where I was visiting him, were to drive all the way to Killington, Vermont, where we would ski with Sondra and Barry. I was staying with Steve in a hotel in town as we were just beginning to become intimate together. In the morning I had my usual difficult time in the bathroom but experienced nothing out of the ordinary. We had some breakfast, threw our bags in the back of his car, and set off. We hadn't driven far before I had to run into a gas-station bathroom. I was shocked at the sight of the bright red blood that filled the toilet bowl, shocked and horrified. I pulled on my jeans and ran into Steve's car dumbfounded. I must have been white as a sheet as I managed to get out the words that something awful had happened. To my absolute surprise, Steve asked me if I had started bleeding. He always had an uncanny way of sensing what was going on with me. We talked about what to do and decided to continue with our journey in the hope that the bleeding would stop. To our dismay the situation was very much the reverse and we were stopping as gas stations the entire way to Vermont.

By the time we arrived at the hotel I had lost a lot of blood. I felt weak, drained, and discouraged. Sondra and Barry had not yet arrived and so we sat patiently in our hotel room waiting. When they finally arrived I told Barry about what had happened. "You probably just popped a hemorrhoid," Barry said. "It happens all the time." "Can that produce a good deal of blood?" I asked. "Absolutely," Barry answered. "Are you experiencing much pain?" "Nothing out of the ordinary," I answered. "Then let's go skiing," said Barry.

Steve and I shared an anxious look. Maybe I should be more descriptive, I thought, but then I could be overreacting. I decided to refrain from further explanation and try to pull myself together. Once at the lodge and outfitted with skis, Sondra and Barry disappeared and Steve and I headed for a lift line. Extreme weakness overtook me, and I felt unable to control my legs. I started slipping backward and glided into a woman who supported me while Steve rushed over. He managed to maneuver my dead-weight body to a chair inside the lodge. We eventually found a ride back to our hotel room, where I slid between the sheets of the bed, warming my body with as many blankets as we could find. It was there I remained as we waited for Barry to return.

When Barry arrived and took my pulse, he looked as if he'd seen a ghost. Immediate plans were made for our return home. By the time we arrived home the bleeding had stopped, however, I spent the next two weeks in the hospital. The same old tests were run, producing practically the same results. It seemed impossible to all of us that the X rays could be exactly the same when the symptoms were so much worse.

Upon my release, Dr. Marvin decided to start me on a new drug that he felt might have a dramatic effect upon my disease. He explained that he hadn't yet introduced cortisone because it is a very powerful drug, and is accompanied by some side effects. Although my X rays didn't indicate a worsening of my condition, a hemorrhage and my testimony did. He felt that the drug was warranted now. He didn't elaborate about the side effects and, at the time, I wasn't particularly interested in hearing about them. I figured that if the drug could handle the disease, I could handle the drug. When the doctor handed me the prescription, he said that he thought I might start feeling a good deal better in a few days. I was hopeful.

I never experienced one day of improvement from the cortisone. The disease seemed to have an uncontrollable hold on me. It wasn't until Steve remarked in early December that I looked like a chipmunk that I noticed how round and distorted my face had become. The first side effect of the drug (moon-face) was surfacing. Beyond the side effects--which grew to include unwanted facial hair, insomnia, and severe depression--the drug had no effect.

I was so terribly ill the evening of my sister's wedding that it is a wonder I ever made it down the aisle as her maid of honor. So much time and energy were spent to make this night perfect and I could hardly bear it. My mother wore that worried look under her smile every time she glanced in my direction.

I spent most of Sondra's wedding night in a hotel room. As I lay in bed thinking of the party going on downstairs, I realized that my illness was taking over my life. Even the splendor of my sister's wedding had been trampled on.

Sondra's wedding was a turning point in my illness. Before, I was sometimes able to poke my head out from inside the clouds and see the sky; now the disease seemed to pervade everything. I could no longer ignore it or sweep it under the rug. The symptoms were too constant, the pain too great.

Shortly after Sondra's wedding we were visited by a friend of my father's. Keith Gonsalves, a charming British gentleman who lived on Grand Bahama Island, was associated with my father through business. During his visit he made a point of telling me about two of his friends who had been cured of arthritis by a healer who resided in England. He said that the healer was referred to as "the man in the sanctuary," and that he had no physical contact with his friends. The healing took place trans-atlantically, so to speak. Now I had always liked Keith very much, and I didn't think he would lie to me. However, at eighteen I was certain that I knew just about everything there was to know about life, and there was no way I was going to believe such ridiculous tales. I held firmly to the belief that medical science was the only sound way to pursue health.

The beginning of 1969 found us very desperate. That is probably what prompted the extreme action we took next. On the advice of Steve's mother, we made contact with a doctor in Manhattan. We were told that Dr. Leon had a marvelous reputation for handling intestinal problems and was noted for curing cancer of the colon. We still couldn't accept the notion that medical science wouldn't cure my illness. After one entire year of treatment by Dr. Marvin, my condition was certainly deteriorating. Didn't we owe it to ourselves to make sure that we had covered all the bases?

A couple of weeks later my mother took me out of school and we drove together into Manhattan in search of new answers. Dr. Leon's office was filled with old, sick-looking people. For a moment I wondered what I was doing there, but the reason was all too clear. I was probably sicker than all of them. When I was finally taken to see Dr. Leon, I was sweaty and shaky. I feared that he would put me through all the same miserable tests again. I was relieved to discover that he didn't feel the need to do his own rectal examination, and was content to read my X rays, press on my stomach, and ask me questions. He seemed quite cheerful as he went about examining me. When I asked if he had actually cured colon cancer, he replied that that had been his father. I envisioned his father with a small magic potion that he kept locked away in a closet. A simple little potion. You drink it and you're cured! Would he, I wondered, share it with me now?

When Dr. Leon told us his idea, I was intrigued. He prescribed a liquid medicine that he wanted me to take a half hour before meals. He claimed that it would coat my intestines, preventing food from further irritating them, thus allowing them to heal. He said that he wanted me to continue all the other medications

I was taking, and simply add this one to the herd. It sounded easy enough. He then gave me a shot of vitamin B12. As he withdrew the needle from my arm, he looked at my mother and said, "You'll need lead shoes to keep her down now!" It sounded good. It meant nothing. As my mother drove sadly and hopefully home through the Lincoln Tunnel, I slept, my head resting on her lap.

Naive as we were, we were not prepared for Dr. Marvin's reaction. He had seemed annoyed when we asked him for my X rays, but he was outraged at the idea of this new medicine. As far as he was concerned, it was unorthodox, unheard of, and he didn't even know what it was made of. None of his colleagues (who were among the most respected doctors in the field) would use such a potion in their practice and neither would he. He said there was no way he could go along with this, and that if I insisted on taking the new medicine, he would be forced to resign from my case.

We were in a quandary. We had come to trust Dr. Marvin. He was kind and caring and we felt close to him. More important, he trusted me. He responded to my complaints sympathetically and without judgment. I did not fully realize what a nice doctor he was. But all of this paled beside the truth, that my condition had grown progressively worse over the year, and maybe it was time for another doctor.

To this day I have never tasted anything so vile as Dr. Leon's magic potion. As I washed the taste away with a gulp of water, I prayed that the magic would do its trick. Well, it sure did something, but the trick was on me. After three days, my pain became more and more severe. My mother and I spent our days trying to get through to Dr. Leon's office, but the phone lines were constantly busy. By the time six days had passed, my abdomen was so distended that I looked as though I was nine months pregnant, and we were still unable to reach our doctor.

We called Barry. Whenever we didn't know where to turn, we called Barry. He and Sondra were living in a two-bedroom apartment just outside of Milburn Center, a ten-minute drive from our house. He said that he would stop by and see me that evening before going home from work. My mother and I realized how absolutely necessary his presence was, for in truth, he was now the only doctor on the case.

By the time Barry arrived my father was home. "What so you think, Bar?" my father asked. With a doctor for a son-in-law, my father was beginning to think he was a doctor, too. "It must be a blockage, right?"

Barry wasn't sure, but he didn't like what he saw. He said that he was afraid that I may have perforated, in which case surgery would be necessary. I didn't know what perforate meant, but I figured that it meant that something inside of me had popped or ripped open. He said that he would have to take some X rays to be absolutely sure, but that one thing was certain. I was going to the hospital. I was disheartened. The thought of returning to that environment for even one minute gnawed away at me. I had no choice, Barry explained. X rays had to be taken.

Barry phoned his uncle, Dr. David Baum, and asked him to please meet us at the hospital. David, a surgeon of extraordinary talent and dedication, was a small, quiet likable man. Since the time of Sondra and Barry's engagement, David had become an affectionate family member and seemed to have a special soft spot in his heart for me. Maybe because he knew I was sick, or maybe he just plain liked me, but he always had a warm word for me and an extra hug. I always had appreciated his presence whenever the family got together and was comforted by the fact that he was a doctor. I was glad to know that he would be meeting us at the hospital.

After reading the X rays, both David and Barry thought that surgery might be indicated but they weren't certain. They wanted the opinion of a gastroenterologist before they made any moves. "We're just surgeons," Barry said. "We're not as qualified to read these X rays as a gastroenterologist is. They've read so many more of these than we have. We have to be sure." Barry and my father headed to the telephones to track down a gastroenterologist.

Naturally, they first tried to locate Dr. Marvin, who was obviously the most familiar with the case and would probably take me back as a patient, considering my predicament. To our dismay, we discovered that he was out of town on vacation, and would not return for another week. Then, on the advice of Barry and David, contact was made with Dr. Larry Timmons, the one doctor who should be glad that his name has been changed in this book. He showed up at the hospital about thirty minutes later. He was a tall slender man with pockmarked skin and dark brown piercing eyes. He looked at me accusingly, disappeared to read the X rays, and then arrogantly announced that surgery was not necessary. In a cold, hard, authoritative tone, he said that the new medication I was taking had obviously caused a blockage, which would disperse of its own, now that I was no longer taking the medicine.

About this he was correct. About everything else he was dead wrong. He immediately sized up my situation and decided that what we had here was the typical case of the spoiled, indulged child who was having a good time at everyone else's expense.

He checked me into the hospital, naturally against my wishes. He then proceeded to embarrass me by giving me a rectal examination in front of five young male interns. He then, with a cold and harsh expression on his face, told me that he knew what I was up to. He said that quite obviously I could fool my mother, my father, and my boyfriend, but that I'd better watch out, because I couldn't fool him. He dismissed all my complaints as exaggerations, treating me with less respect than I would give an animal. On top of all my physical pain, I now felt completely abused and humiliated.

This was the most uncomfortable hospital stay I'd had yet. Along with Dr. Timmons's cruelty, I was much sicker. Every test and examination irritated my sore insides even more than they had before. Dr. Timmons ordered an entire X-ray series, which included the night-before laxative and the morning enema. The enema was not only an embarrassment now but a painful experience as well. I remember the anger rising in my chest as the nurses on my floor made fun of me, referring to me as a mama's baby, as I called out for my mother in fear and pain. Later, lying on the cold, hard X-ray table, I felt unbelievably small and humiliated, unable to get used to the experience of a barium enema. I could not get through the sigmoidoscopy without a shot of Demerol. Now that I think of it, it was a rare occurrence when I survived the day without a shot of Demerol.

My mother seemed to go through every painful experience with me, from the changing of the IV needle, to the daily blood tests, to the painkilling injections. We were somehow locked in this thing together, the situation bringing us closer all the time. While my father, Steve, Sondra and Barry, as well as my grandparents frequently visited my hospital room, it was my mother who spent an eternity with me. After a Demerol injection, we would engage in long conversations. I would become extremely talkative. We were more like friends than mother and daughter. More than that, we were like two lost friends, trying to find a light at the end of a very dark and ominous tunnel. Led always by an eternal optimism, we kept searching for an answer, a reprieve...anything.

The new set of X rays showed very little change. How could the disease feel so much worse, and yet not appear worse when X-rayed? I was depressed, and what was worse, this news fit Dr. Timmons's warped opinion of me. He now knew, as he unkindly expressed, that I had a mild case of ileitis, because the X rays showed that a six-inch segment of small bowel was affected. He also knew that such a mild case could in no way produce the pain that I was complaining about. The time had come for me to shape up and stop driving everyone crazy. While we were all growing to hate Dr. Timmons, we had no guarantee that Dr. Marvin would take the case back and we couldn't imagine starting all over again with a new doctor.

Upon my release from the hospital I was sicker, weaker, and thinner than ever. Steve's visits became more important to me, while my sister and Barry were daily confidants.

Dr. Timmons decided to test me for ulcers and kidney problems. He found nothing wrong with my kidneys but decided to treat me for ulcers, just in case. For this, he prescribed an ounce of milk every hour. This was extremely shocking to my mother and me, as I had been denied milk and all milk products since the day ileitis had been diagnosed.

Twenty-four hours later I began to hemorrhage massively. There is no way of knowing whether the milk treatment was involved in bringing on the bleeding. My hunch is that I had it coming anyway, but the milk certainly couldn't have helped. Needless to say, the scene was terrifying. Again, the hemorrhage took the form of severe diarrhea, the only difference being that what poured out of me relentlessly was my own blood. At approximately two A.M. Dr. Baum arrived, took one look at the bright red blood in the toilet bowl, and explained that we had no choice but to check me into the hospital immediately.

The doctors began immediate blood transfusions in the hope of making me strong enough to withstand surgery. Doctors Baum and Mankowitz felt certain now that the only recourse was to go inside and remove the diseased portions of my bowel.

Up until now surgery had always seemed like an easy way out, if all else failed. I had grown used to hearing Barry say, "A chance to cut is a chance to cure". But now, with the prospect of surgery so near, I began to wonder about the pain involved, realizing that I might get more than I had bargained for. Oddly enough, I had no concerns about dying. I assumed that I would live, but my concern was steadily growing about what I would feel like when I came out of surgery. Panic began to set in. I had a dread fear of pain. I began asking everyone around me if it was going to hurt, receiving my only answer from a friend of the family who was also a doctor. Stanley, who practiced gynecology, happened to be in the hospital and stopped in my room when he heard I had been admitted.

"Well, Sher," he said, "you know that when you cut your finger it hurts a little. You have to understand that this will be a somewhat deeper cut than a finger scratch. Naturally it will hurt some, but you'll be given something for the pain." At this point I knew that I was in for trouble.

The next few hours were spent getting me ready for surgery. I was in a state of complete terror, but was trying very hard to be strong. My parents and sister wiped my head and held my hands as the bag of blood, suspended above us on an IV pole, reminded us of the inevitable. Dr. Timmons arrived. A catheter was inserted into my bladder and my nightgown was cut away so as not to disturb my intravenous needles.

All that I could do was wonder about the pain. Could I bear it? I had had some pretty stiff pain, but I had the unerring sense that I hadn't seen nothin' yet. A few moments later I was rolled onto a stretcher, and before I knew what was happening, I was being swiftly wheeled down a corridor. My mother's hand was clasped tightly inside my own. She kept pace with the stretcher, her face glued to mine as she accompanied me as far as she was allowed. We parted ways at the big green doors marked "Operating Rooms -- No Admittance." My mother bent over and kissed me. Then the ominous big green doors opened to admit me and I was wheeled away.

I lay on the stretcher for a while. I was a little groggy from sedation, but I knew what was going on. I saw other stretchers lining the hallways, also equipped with patients who were lying quietly. I was alone. Fear rose up inside of me, only partially subdued by the medication. "Why am I alone?" I thought. "Why can't my mother be here with me?"

A few minutes later I was wheeled into a room. A group of doctors and nurses helped me to maneuver my body off the stretcher and onto the table. "Where is David?" I thought. As I turned my head I saw him walking toward me. "David!" I said. "I'm scared, David." "I know you are," he answered. "Hold my hand, please, David," I said. As the anesthesiologist announced that he was inserting sodium pentathol into the IV in my arm, David told me that I was going to have a nice restful sleep soon. I quickly looked around the room and saw Barry's face. "Thank God," I thought, another source of security and comfort. "Count backward from one hundred, Sheri," David said. I don't remember much past ninety-seven.

Anesthesia is an odd thing. You can be under for hours, and yet at the first inkling of awareness, it feels as if no time has elapsed at all. I have this vague memory of feeling something inside my throat and a voice saying, "Well, she's coming to, better close her up." I don't know if I had become semi-conscious during surgery, or if that was a dream. What I do know for certain is what I felt like as my senses began to come back to me in the recovery room. I felt as if the entire earth was sitting upon my abdomen. I never knew such pain could be possible, let alone endurable. "Oh, my God," I thought, "I don't think I can deal with this." It hurt to move my toe. It hurt to move my pinkie. My mouth was incredibly dry and my throat hurt. My head throbbed, while my abdominal pain was beyond imagination. I kept trying to go back to sleep, hoping to escape through dreams, but the pain kept jutting into my awareness.

Within a few minutes my mother was at my side. I could feel her pain almost as acutely as I could feel my own. I don't think I have ever loved her more than at that moment. The sight of her gave me courage. Her love convinced me, without words, that I would be able to stand all that I had to in order to get well. Her presence willed me to live. What a powerful and wonderful force love is!

My mother explained to me that Dr. Timmons had apologized. He had walked out of the OR in the middle of the surgery and announced to the members of my family that he had been wrong, that the surgery proved I had a far more extensive case of ileitis than the X rays had ever revealed. I felt enormous satisfaction hearing this. "You see," my mother said, "your illness was extensive and there was real reason for your pain. Now that it has all finally been removed you are going to heal."

Although my mother did not mention this to me, Dr. Timmons also stated, rather abruptly, that Dr. Baum had to consider whether to perform an ileostomy. My family was shocked. Although they knew very little about ileostomies, they did know that it meant wearing an appliance on my body for the collection of waste materials. They couldn't imagine how I would ever adjust to such a situation and were greatly relieved to hear that Dr. Baum had decided to perform a resection instead. (In the case of the latter, the diseased portions of the bowel are removed, the healthy pieces are joined, and the bowel is reconnected normally.) Although in retrospect I realize that Dr. Timmons meant to inform my family of what was taking place in the OR, during what turned out to be a four-and-a-half-hour surgery, he only frightened my family further.

The next few days were a haze of pain and discomfort. I spent one night in intensive care in which I was aware of other beds around the room, some enclosed in oxygen tents. I heard people crying and begging for painkillers and I found myself trying to find the strength to do the same. It seemed as though the nurses' only reply was that I wasn't due for a shot for another two hours. I'd just have to wait. "Just wait?" I thought. "How could I wait?" Each minute of pain seemed like an eternity. I watched the clock on the wall endlessly, always amazed that more time hadn't elapsed. When the nurse finally came to my bedside with a needle, pulling myself over on my side to expose my backside was agony. Ah, but after those first few minutes, when the drug takes effect and the pain begins to dull, you know it has all been worth it, and you relish whatever relief you are given.

I remember that as soon as I was settled in a private room, my mother came and told me that Steve, who had been staying around the hospital waiting to see me, wanted to see me now. Sick as I was, the first thing that I thought of was the huge clump of knots that had formed in the back of my long brown hair during all the sweating, tossing, and turning of the last two days. We had tried to comb it out but it looked as though we would have to cut it. I decided that I looked terrible and that I didn't want to be seen in such a state. I needed to see Steve, but couldn't bear the thought of shocking him. "No," I told my mother, "tell him he can't come in. Tell him I don't want him to see me like this."

My mother left the room to give Steve my message, but returned immediately. Steve was not about to stand for any of this. "He wants to come in," she said. "He loves you, he wants to see you." A moment later Steve stood by my bed, gently stroking my hair, assuring me that I never looked more beautiful than at that moment. There was no question in my mind that I was loved.

I had severe discomfort in my throat and ear from a tube going into my right nostril and down my throat. My nurse explained that this Levine tube drained the bile and bodily fluids, which my intestines presently could not digest. It is, in actuality, a very helpful, and in many cases necessary tool in recovery from bowel surgery, but at this point my only interest in it was to get it out! My ear and throat throbbed continuously, and I was allowed only an occasional ice chip for the dryness. My doctors told me that the tube couldn't be removed, nor could I have anything to drink until I began to pass gas or have bowel movements, which could take a few days. I couldn't believe that we were all sitting around waiting for me to fart. Physiological functions had always been a private matter to me. Now mine were the business of the entire seventh-floor nurses' station!

My family practically lived in the hospital along with Steve, who came to see me every day. Flowers came by the cartful, with telegrams and gifts galore, but this was one time I couldn't muster a smile.

Each day I was experiencing increasingly worse gas pains. From what I was told, I understood that David had done a lot of cutting into my intestines in order to remove the disease. because the disease was not isolated but was spread throughout my intestines in patches, David had to cut, remove, and sew back together all the healthy tissue that remained. Therefore many places in my intestines were swollen as a result of cutting and stitching. This made even the slightest act of functioning difficult. The pain was unnerving. David explained to me that painkillers, while valuable in one way, could also hurt my progress in another. They slowed down bowel function and could delay the time in which my bowels would work again. So, in essence, he was telling me to take as little pain medicine as possible and bear as much of the pain as I could.

Finally, on the seventh day I began to pass gas. We practically passed out flyers throughout the hall! I felt enormous relief, physically and mentally, as I now assumed that I was on my way to recovering, and putting all of this misery behind me.

Once the Levine tube was removed, I was going to walk down the hall with my nurse and actually take a bath! I would still be connected to an IV pole, but that didn't compare to the relief of being free of the catheter and Levine tube. The very thought of immersing my sore, sweaty body in warm caressing water sounded wonderful. The pleasure, however, was short-lived. When I returned to bed I began to experience bad cramps again. My intestines, for whatever reason, stopped functioning and I began to feel nauseated. Five minutes later, I was throwing up and running a fever. Barry and David were alarmed, and I was distraught. Down went the Levine tube--it's much less fun when you're awake--and immediate X rays were ordered.

Fortunately, the X rays showed that nothing had gone wrong with the surgery. My present difficulties were the result of an infection and I was spared the agony of another operation. Yet I can't really say that things were looking up. I had severe abdominal cramps. The Levine tube felt as if it were burning a hole in my neck and ear. I was weak beyond belief, and I was sore and aching from head to toe. But "Thank God," I thought, "at least I don't have to go into surgery again."

The next few days were a long and tiresome waiting game. We had to wait until the antibiotics killed the infection enough for my bowels to begin to work again. Then and then alone could the Levine tube be removed, and I be allowed a little bit of water. How I wanted water.

As the days passed I watched a lot of television. The image that remains clearest in my mind from all the hours of TV is from a soft-drink ad--A bottle of soda sitting in the center of a cool stream of rushing water. I couldn't tell which looked more refreshing, the stream or the bottle. I longed to devour them both. I'll never forget what it feels like to be so thirsty and not have the freedom to take a drink. To this day it is a great pleasure for me to take a glass, fill it to the brim with ice, pour cool refreshing liquid over the ice, and drink it to my heart's content. It was then that I learned that the simple pleasures of life, which are usually taken for granted, come into sharp focus when they are taken away.

Once my bowels began to work I was in for another kind of trouble. I had intense diarrhea and could barely get off the bed to use the portable commode by the bedside. Moving my body still caused great pain. I had a bad case of hemorrhoids, and I could barely use my own hands to clean myself because they were all rigged up to IV needles. With one nurse to hold me and another to clean me, I felt completely humiliated and small. But basically, things had taken a step in the right direction. With great relief I gave up the Levine tube and was allowed small amounts of liquids. With great effort I went for small walks down the hall and sat up in a chair. Steve and I engaged in Dr. Timmons jokes, the resulting laughter creating as much pain as pleasure. The general tone in my flower-cluttered room was improving as my situation seemed to move out of the critical stages.

The two months discussed in this chapter seemed to me like two years. Therefore it was only natural that when I was drinking, eating, and using the bathroom frequently, but without pain, I started to grow anxious to go home. Doctors Baum and Mankowitz agreed, and signed the release form. Dr. Timmons took a little more persuading, but eventually he gave in.

I felt as if I'd been let out of prison on the warm sunny morning that I left the hospital in Newark. I had been admitted on a cool winter's night, and during my stay, without my awareness of it, winter had mysteriously turned into spring. And what a glorious spring day it was. Everywhere was green, everything smelled sweet, freedom never felt so good!

My dog Mitzy, who my mother said faithfully checked the house throughout the day for my presence, returning always to my bedroom, was delighted to see me as we both climbed into my soft luscious pink canopy bed. It was good to be home. Although I was still quite weak, it seemed as though the ileitis disease had actually been removed. The daily pain was gone, and although I still had to make frequent bathroom visits, I was no longer suffering. I weighed a mere sixty pounds and was covered with black and blue bruises from the enormous number of shots and intravenous needles. But that would all change. The illness was gone and the hellish ordeal was behind me.

Chapter Two

The Trauma Continues

It wasn't until I was home and life was getting back to normal, that I learned of the severity of my operation and of the type of surgery that had been considered for me and decided against by Dr. Baum. Sondra explained that David, who is known for his calm and quiet manner, found himself in an emotional state that was almost overwhelming. Shocked to discover such extensive bowel disease inside me, he was faced with the serious decision to perform either an ileostomy or a resection. Sondra explained that in the case of an ileostomy, a piece of my intestine would be brought through my abdominal wall and I would eliminate waste through it. Unable to make the decision, Dr. Baum made a phone call in the middle of surgery to an associate of his in Manhattan. Dr. Arnold told David that he was thinking with his heart and not with his mind, and that in his opinion a temporary ileostomy should be performed. (With a temporary ileostomy the rectum remains intact, thus allowing for the reconnection of the bowel at some later date.) I guess because David and I were so close, he could not help but think with his heart, and therefore could not bring himself to perform an ileostomy on me. Thus the resulting surgery was a resection.

How shocking this story sounded to me at the time, and how awful! "I would rather be dead," I told my sister, and believed it to be true. Imagine me walking around with a bag under my clothes collecting waste! I shuddered at the thought.

About two weeks later I started to hemorrhage again. The same old routine, the bloody runs. I was rushed to the hospital, transfusions were set up, and the waiting game was on to see if the bleeding would stop. This time it did, and after a few days I was sent home. We were all very shook up about this, however, as we had thought that my problems were over.

On a trip to the Bahamas with my parents, a vacation David had approved of, I was waiting in the beauty parlor for my mother when a trip to the bathroom confirmed the start of bleeding again. We panicked. To our relief the bleeding stopped within a few hours, but the anxiety remained. The bleeding was alarming and disconcerting, like a time bomb always ticking away. We never could be sure whether it was going to go off again or of the severity of it, if it did. I was supposed to be well--but was I really?

That June I was determined to attend my senior prom with Steve. I felt as if I had been forgotten by all of my classmates and I wanted to make my presence known, to let people know that I still existed. They couldn't understand what I had been going through, though, I reasoned, but at least they could see that I had survived!

My mother, in whose eyes I now was a china doll, was uneasy. She would have preferred it if I didn't move a muscle. She pleaded with me to stay at home and rest and not push myself. "Honey," she said, "let yourself have a chance to heal." She was so upset that I could not have gone with a free heart. I granted her wish and decided to pass on the prom. Unfortunately, my mother's fears were not groundless. She was trying to prevent the inevitable, but then is the inevitable ever preventable?

The very next day, while shopping with my mother and sister in Bloomingdale's, I began to hemorrhage again. After a few trips to the Bloomingdale's bathroom, we nervously made our way to my mother's car, eventually ending up in Dr. Timmon's office. I knew that I was in trouble because I just couldn't stop running to the bathroom. "God," I thought, "just stop this, now! Please!" But my blood rushed through me like a river. And oh, God, I knew what was next. Dr. Timmons said that we had no other choice but to return to the hospital, and this time I didn't even bother to try to convince anyone otherwise.

I knew that more surgery was a strong possibility, given the severity of this hemorrhage. I was doubly concerned now, for I remembered what my sister had told me about ileostomies. It didn't take a hell of a lot of brains to deduce that if I had to go into surgery again, I might very well end up with one. I just didn't know if I could make the adjustment.

At the hospital Dr. Timmons ordered a coagulant, in enema form, in an attempt to try to stop the bleeding, hoping to avoid another surgery. Unfortunately the treatment had no effect and the bleeding continued full force.

Nothing was more obvious to me then than the fact that I wanted to live even if that meant adjusting to an ileostomy--the thought of which still made me shudder. I also realized, at the same time, that I could not allow myself to indulge in too much thought about the ileostomy, for I sensed that I needed all my energy to survive the surgery. It's not as if I consciously realized this, but I somehow knew not to dwell upon it. I tried to summon up all my courage as the emergency preparations were begun to make me ready for my second surgery.

An immediate blood transfusion was started, but this time with greater difficulty. Because my veins were so worn from overuse during my last surgery, Barry could not find a suitable vein to administer the blood through. Therefore he was forced to perform a minor surgical procedure in the crook of my arm, in order to place a needle in a vein deeper than surface level. Everybody around me looked panicky. David stopped in briefly, said he'd see me in the OR, and disappeared into the hall. Everything seemed to be moving too fast. As I was whisked down the corridor to the operating room, my mother running alongside the stretcher, I knew what I was up against. I looked up into my mother's face, my mind teeming with questions. "Mommy, will I be a whole girl when I come out?" I asked. I must have torn a hole in her heart by asking. "Whatever you will be, you will be alive, and you will be beautiful, and you will get well!" she answered.

When I awoke in the recovery room I saw Barry, who was standing just behind the head of my bed. I somehow knew the answer before I asked him if the ileostomy had been done, to which he replied, "Just for a little while, Sher." The pain was as bad as I had remembered it. The dryness in my mouth and irritating Levine tube were present again also. I knew that I was in no way ready to look at my body in its present state; nevertheless I kept picturing it. I couldn't imagine how I would ever adjust. To my mind, the idea of moving one's bowels through one's abdomen was disgusting. I became obsessed with ways to disguise the bag, which I hadn't even looked at yet.

Steve was helpful beyond measure. He came to my bedside, placed his hands on my belly, and said that he could not hate anything that gave me back to him. When many young men would have walked away, he walked in. His parents also lent support, holding to the belief that now my bowel could have the rest that it required. We all maintained that, as soon as it was possible, the ileostomy would be reversed.

My own parents were heartbroken, although they tried not to show it. How this could have happened to their daughter was beyond them. I couldn't imagine how I would ever make the adjustment. My once perfect body, which I had been too young and foolish to appreciate, seemed mutilated. I felt as if I was now marred, in an unforgivable way. Again I sensed the need to ignore this wave of negative thought and reasoning. It was as if a portion of myself, which knew better, fought to pool all of my resources for immediate use. Again this proved very necessary, as the recovery from the second surgery was ever bit as eventful as the recovery from the first.

To begin with, as before, there was a problem with the functioning of my bowel. We were anxious for my bowel to begin working, indicating that the surgery had been successful, and that the hated Levine tube could be removed. Unfortunately, this was not the case and the little plastic bag my nurse had tied around my belly remained empty. There was no sign of the passing of fluids through my body into the bag. Soon I became nauseated.

I remember that my mother and I were in the hospital room with one of my nurses. Periodically throughout the day it would be her job to drain the Levine tube. This entailed using a suction device to draw out any excess fluid, thus assisting the tube in its function. As I became overwhelmed with waves of nausea I told my mother, who in turn told the nurse, who in turn looked at the machine connected to the other end of the Levine tube and answered, "The machine is working."

"Well, it may be working," my mother said, "but my daughter is very nauseous. I think it would be best if you would please drain the tube!"

"No," she answered, "the machine is working!"

My mother grabbed the suction device and a bowl and began to drain the tube herself. She must have filled the bowl up four times with my bodily fluids, affording me enormous relief and warning us that something was not right.

The nurse called for an intern, who, after putting his ear to my stomach, contacted my regular doctors. X rays were then done in my room by a portable machine, because I was considered too weak to be moved. The X rays showed that my intestines had coiled themselves up into some kind of knot and that was why they were not yet able to function.

The next thing I knew, Barry walked into the room briskly with some kind of ball in his hand. I could see that he was trying to press it into as small a shape as possible and then, before I knew what was happening, he pushed it into my one free nostril back as far as he could, saying, "Swallow, swallow, swallow." I felt shocked for an instant and then saw that Barry was feeding a tube, appearing at this point just like a Levine tube, slowly into me. He explained that the ball that was on the end of the tube was a ball of mercury, the weight of which was going to go through my intestines and break up the coil. I was to alternate every half hour from lying on one side to the other, assisting the tube in going through my intestines.

After two hours of turning from side to side, an X ray revealed that the tube had merely coiled into a knot itself, and so the entire process had to be started again. Fortunately, this time it was successful. By the end of the day we began to see fluid passing into the clear plastic bag on my abdomen, which upset me as much as it pleased me. Now, for the first time, I dared to look at this contraption that was my body, and I cringed with shock and dismay. It looked as though I had a red cherry growing out of where my belly button should be, with a clear plastic bag placed over it and tied around my body with a string. I also discovered another red, cherry-like opening lower down on my left side, near my groin, which Barry said was the temporary. I really had no idea what he meant except that, because of it, I could be re-hooked again at some later date.

My mother and I both recall that, at this point, Barry had said something to the effect that there had not been enough large bowel left to make a proper temporary hook-up, and that David had invented an unusual solution in order to make my situation reversible. I didn't understand what he was talking about. The ileostomy was temporary, which meant to me that I would endeavor to get rid of it as soon as possible. Until it was gone, I didn't care to know anything about the details beyond how to live with the situation now.

By this point my bowels were working and the little bag was filling up constantly with my bodily fluids. The nurses took one bag off me, replacing it with another, while I watched, detached from my own body.

My next complication was a high fever. Since my bowels were working, indicating that the surgery had been successful, it was assumed that I had another infection. This time the antibiotic had to be administered by injection, which was what I feared, because of the pain involved. To make matters worse, I would have to have the shot twice a day, and what a shot it was! Barry said it might sting a little as he proceeded to inject me with a serum so painful that I cried for ten minutes. All in all, life just seemed to be one miserable, painful event after another.

It was at this time that a woman came onto my case whose presence was more than helpful. Ruth Kale, a fine postsurgical (as well as general) nurse, was approached by David and asked to take the case, since my current nurse felt that she could no longer stand the pressure. Ruth, who told me herself during an interview I held with her in 1987 (the first time we had seen each other in seventeen years) that she always liked a challenge, came on to the case with zest and determination. She also had a good deal of practical knowledge about ileostomies and was not afraid of getting her hands wet. She informed me, as she entered my room, that she was referred to around the hospital as the shit nurse, because she handled so many of these problems. I felt immediate embarrassment when she said that, but it was obvious that she did not look at my situation as unusual or terrible. Waste to her was a natural part of life, and just something else to be dealt with, where to me it represented something to be ashamed of.

Ruth's attitude, so healthy and accepting, began to set the groundwork for my being able to cope. I knew that soon I was going to have to learn how to take care of this thing myself, and that meant approaching my fear of looking at and touching my body. I had an enormous aversion to it but Ruth didn't. She explained to me that once I had healed from the surgery I would be able to use much nicer appliances that wouldn't be horrendous.

In part I realized that this was me now, that I had to find a way to accept it, and that I could, and that I would. Yet, in another part, I couldn't accept it at all, and I didn't even want to try. I could feel my moods swing back and forth, from one extreme to the other. From feeling sorry for myself, to feeling glad to be alive, I somehow began to set myself off in the direction of accepting my present reality.

I was also greatly relieved to discover that Ruth, who had a special skill for giving injections, could administer my antibiotic painlessly. It was really just a matter of taking a little more time, which I realize most doctors and nurses don't have. A terrible ordeal became an ordinary event. Believe it or not, my uncle Bernie drove Ruth back to the hospital every evening to administer the medication during another nurse's shift, because nobody could do it like Ruth. At this point, it seemed as though every member of my family would have done anything to save me from pain.

I was surprised to learn from Ruth that, on the day she walked in on my case that neither she or the doctors felt that I would pull through, and that Dr. Baum expressed his concern to her often. "It's a good thing," my mother said (also present at the interview), "that he didn't tell me what he was thinking."

For my next act, I developed a frightening complication. It was frightening because my doctors were not certain as to the cause of my alarming symptoms. According to Ruth my blood pressure was dropping, my hemoglobin was down, my fever had shot up, and the doctors were afraid for my survival. My mother said that this remains in her mind as the most terrifying of all the times of my illness because she was beginning to feel that we just might lose the fight. She saw real fear in the doctors' faces, and she felt that I was losing my sense of reality.

Once blood tests were run and analyzed the mystery was solved. I had developed an electrolyte imbalance due to excessive fluid loss through the ileostomy. Apparently when my bowels began to work, they worked overtime. We, however, did not know what to expect from my bowels and, therefore, no one was aware that I was losing too much fluid. Now that we realized the cause of my problem, another IV was inserted into a vein in my shoulder and the necessary electrolytes were administered.

That night, at my request, I was given some strong medication and I finally slept through the night. When I awoke in the morning I felt a good deal better. My mother seemed genuinely shocked when I told her how much better I felt. I could not understand why she seemed so surprised. At the time I had no notion of what my family was going through. As difficult as reality was, to my mind death was not a possibility. The main issue to me was when the suffering would stop.

I came through this last complication and began to heal. I was now faced with the difficult task of adjusting to the ileostomy and yet, at this point, the actual fight for survival came to an end.

Learning to accept and adjust to the ileostomy was no easy task. Ruth Kale was vitally helpful. She touched my body and the fluids came out of it without any hesitation or sense of disgust. She was as natural and comfortable with it as I would have been petting a puppy. Her attitude demonstrated to me that I didn't have to be afraid of what I was, and that my squeamishness could be overcome, but I knew it wasn't going to be easy.

Finally, I was released from the hospital. Although incredibly thin and worn, I was alive, and relieved to be out of pain. I began to recover my strength quickly in my home environment. Steve was unbelievably wonderful as he showered me with gifts and affection. Truly he helped, almost more than anyone, to make my adjustment bearable. The fact that he remained my boyfriend, refusing to run away from the situation, was positive proof that I was still desirable. He was much less squeamish about the ileostomy than I was. He clearly didn't seem offended. To me his attitude seemed nearly unbelievable. I was so narrow-minded at eighteen, so prissy and set in my ways, that I couldn't imagine physically loving someone who was in my situation. How he could continue to love me was a mystery to me. My attitude toward myself had changed radically. I now looked down on myself as someone unworthy.

I was in enormous emotional pain, which I tried to conceal.

On the surface it looked as if I was doing okay, making the necessary adjustments and continuing with my life. Underneath, however, there was a profound sadness. I was determined not to let it show. I acted as if I were much less upset than I was. I even advised other ostomates on how to get back on their feet, physically and emotionally, and yet I had not done so myself. As I look back on it now, helping others and pretending that I wasn't so miserable made my adjustment easier. Clearly, I wasn't yet ready to face the enormous shock and hurt feelings that resided just below the surface level. Although I was aware that I was sad and disappointed, it was not until years later that the deep wounds inflicted by my illness were acknowledged and allowed to heal.

I was very fortunate that my schoolteachers and principal decided to graduate me and, with a little help from my guidance counselor, I was accepted by a local university. This way I could attend college in the fall and still live at home. The idea of living at home didn't thrill me, but I didn't know how I could share a bathroom with other girls. I couldn't imagine telling other people that I had an ileostomy, or worse, having them see it.

At this point my mother, sister, and I spent what seemed to be an eternity in the bathroom trying to get an appliance on me that felt comfortable. We were unaware that I had a constriction problem (my abdominal wall grew tighter and tighter around the exposed piece of intestine, called the stoma), and therefore interpreted the constant itching I experienced as the result of an ill-fitting appliance. We tried everything we could think of to make me more comfortable. We were constantly taking the appliance on and off, adjusting the fit, and applying different creams and ointments. However, within a short time after leaving the bathroom, I became very uncomfortable.

At this point my operation was a deep, dark secret that I confided only to one friend besides Steve. Even my younger brothers were kept in the dark, as my parents shared my belief that my operation was not something to be talked about. After a while, my brothers began to wonder what my mother and I were doing in the bathroom all of the time. Eventually I sat down and explained the situation to Richard, who, like everyone else, accepted it better than I did.

As soon as possible, I made trips with my mother to Philadelphia to see a gastroenterologist chosen by Dr. Baum, to consult on when to go back into surgery to close the bowel. We made three visits, and I was subjected to some of my very "favorite" tests.

I clearly remember the jealousy I felt as my mother and I traveled home from Philly in early June, stuck in bumper-to-bumper traffic while carfuls of young people drove to the Woodstock festival. How I envied them and their freedom to be on their own without parents and doctors. Although my illness insulated me from the minds of other young people throughout the country, I nevertheless sensed something in the air. It was clear in the music I listened to, and I wanted a taste of it. In my own quiet way, I felt a part of the movement.

I spent the summer regaining my strength and weight, lounging around the pool in my parents' home, and going out with Steve.

I was pleased when he decided to spend his junior year in Manhattan, at NYU, as part of an exchange program. I felt safe knowing he would be around. Steve rented a small apartment in Greenwich Village, (which has always been my favorite part of Manhattan), and with the prospect of reconnective surgery in the future, life seemed better.

Although I was very uncomfortable about having sex, and extremely ill at ease about taking my clothes off, Steve and I did have an intimate relationship. He was patient and understanding with me, loving and supportive. He was just what I needed, which made it all the more difficult for me to accept what happened next.

In the early fall Steve informed me that he needed to date other women. Fear rocked my body as I listened to his justifications. My emotions raced from rage to sadness, to disbelief, to fear, and I begged Steve to reconsider. I knew that he loved me and I hoped to play on his sympathies, but Steve was unshakable. Naturally, I was certain that his new attitude had to do with the ileostomy. Although he tried to convince me otherwise, I couldn't believe him.

I was scared, annoyed, bored, disinterested, and upset when I drove into the parking lot of Drew University for freshman orientation. I had no idea what I was doing there. I missed Steve terribly. I was afraid to date other men, knowing that they would eventually want to get sexual and I would have to tell them about my body. I couldn't bear another rejection, and I couldn't imagine that it wouldn't come about. I just wanted to go to sleep and wake up in the morning to find that it had been a dream.

Fortunately, I began to develop friendships with some of the local kids who, like myself, had not gone away to school. That created a social outlet for me and saved me from dealing with the pressure of dating. It helped my self-confidence to be socializing with people my own age.

Sometime during this fall my gastroenterologist announced that my bowel appeared to be healed and that now seemed as good a time as any to reconnect it. He explained that if the surgery was not successful, I would have to accept a permanent ileostomy, but that at this point in time we should hope for the best.

I was very excited as my mother and I stopped off at my father's office on the way home from Philadelphia to give him the news. To my surprise, my father was not very pleased at the prospect of my facing another surgery and said so. I was shocked and disappointed that he didn't share my enthusiasm.

Nevertheless, I was headstrong and headed over to David's home that evening to tell him the good news. My heart sank when David said that he refused to do the surgery at this time. "You just aren't well enough," he said, "and I don't believe that your body can withstand another surgery right now."

I couldn't believe my ears. Furthermore, I was outraged that he had sent me to a specialist, had allowed me to go through so many dreaded examinations, if he didn't intend to operate anyway. As I drove home I was sad and disillusioned, but I also felt a surge of relief. Could it be that I wasn't really ready to face another surgery yet?

Things did continue to improve in some ways. Steve was having a hard time with our separation. He began to pursue me actively again. This time, though, I wanted some assurances. I felt that I needed some kind of formal commitment and pressured Steve for one.

We became engaged, and planned to be married in early August. Both our families were very excited. Steve and I became so caught up that I don't really think we knew exactly what was happening. It seemed like the right thing to do. He didn't want to lose me, and I didn't want to face life alone, without him. We were both so young and had been through so much together that no other course of action seemed possible.

I felt free now to drop out of college, which was something I had wanted to do desperately. I found school tedious, and my courses difficult to concentrate upon. The only thing that seemed truly interesting to me was what I referred to as my new pot-smoking awareness. In keeping with my generation, I became very introspective and involved in discovering more about myself, my thoughts and my motives. I began to feel that I had to understand myself in order to understand what was happening around me. I started reading books about psychology, trying different theories on for size, to see which ones seemed valid.

Such pondering kept my mind active, while on a physical level I had plenty to do planning my wedding and engagement party. I no longer suffered pain, had fairly abundant energy, and outside of my annoying constriction problems, I seemed to be well. I smoked pot frequently and the marijuana slowed down my digestive process, which decreased the amount of trips I had to make to the bathroom, and increased my weight. I also discovered that pot distracted me from the constant itching that resulted from the constriction problem. Distraction, however, didn't solve the problem.

Two days before my engagement party my constriction problem made itself truly felt. We were expecting nearly two hundred people for a party at my parents' home when I suddenly got a case of the runs so severe that by that evening I was flat on my back. Dr. Baum came by and, to my dismay, tried to put his pinkie into the opening of the stoma and found that it was practically closed shut. My abdominal wall was growing together around the stoma, and thus I was experiencing severe fluid loss. The doctor explained that the diarrhea was a direct result of this partial blockage. The only way to stop the problem was to go into surgery and cut the overgrown skin away. He said that it would most likely be a minor surgical procedure. However, if for some reason he was not able to solve the problem from the outside, he would be forced to completely open me up again, which would qualify as major surgery. "Major surgery again?" I thought, "Please God not that!" And what, I wondered, were we going to do about the party?

We came up with an outrageous solution. That night Barry arrived at out home with an IV pole and all the equipment necessary to set up intravenous therapy for me in my bedroom. The plan was to replace all of the fluids I had lost while a strong constipating drug called parapectolin would be used to block the diarrhea condition until after the party. Then I would have the surgery. We had two days to get me into shape for the party, and we succeeded triumphantly. I looked healthy and fresh as a daisy, and when the guests arrived, no one would have thought that I had spent the last two days in bed.

The party went nicely from what I could tell, but as the day wore on I became more and more apprehensive about the impending surgery. I elected to discontinue the parapectolin because it made me drowsy, and within no time the diarrhea returned. By the time the last guest had left, I looked quite different from the way I had looked when the party began. Huge hollows appeared in my cheeks as my strength began to wane. I climbed into my bed and thought about the next day. I was looking at another surgery, the extent of which would remain a mystery until the actual event.

The moment that I opened my eyes in the recovery room, I knew that the surgery had been a minor one because I had minimal pain and I had no Levine tube in my nose. I breathed more than a sigh of relief!

In order to prevent future surgeries of this nature, Barry told me to dilate the stoma every day when changing the appliance. This meant putting my pinkie into the opening of the stoma and keeping it there for a few minutes. In this way I would be pushing the skin outward and working against the constriction process. The doctors said that they hoped this would work, and that if it didn't, we would just have to operate again. Sounded great to me!

Steve and I were excited about our upcoming wedding. My parents were planning a huge affair with six hundred people. We chose the Pierre Hotel in Manhattan and selected an elaborate meal. We were starting fittings for our gowns and the invitations were just about to be mailed when I surprised myself and my parents by announcing that I wanted something smaller and simpler. I said that I felt that such an enormous wedding was a waste of money. I was very outspoken and didn't realize at the time that I disappointed and hurt my parents. I was putting down their style and way of doing things. During the next few years, I became more and more critical of their values. I blamed them for my own confusion. I was quick to criticize what I saw as their materialistic values, but I had no problem about taking their money.

This was a difficult time for me. As I delved more deeply into psychology, I began to blame my past for my present difficulties. It was easy then to transfer the blame to my parents. It was only natural then for me to desire change, but I was unduly critical of them. You could say that I fit into my generation well, as all around me, young people bitched and complained about the world their parents had created.

Both sets of parents were disturbed by Steve's and my behavior, but they agreed to go along with our plans. Looking back, I'm not sure that it mattered to Steve which wedding plan we followed, but I clearly wanted an event that reflected my changing values. As a result, the guest list was limited to a hundred people. Half of these were kids, which really limited our parents in the amount of people they could invite. Steve and I made our own invitations sporting a photograph of the two of us on the front. Inside we quoted Crosby, Stills, and Nash -- "One person two alone three together for each other" --- and one of my grandmothers wanted to know if it meant that I was pregnant. We wrote our own vows, and I bought myself an old-fashioned lacy dress in Greenwich Village. I was undoubtedly rude and arrogant, but I rejoiced in the feeling of running my own life.

We went apartment hunting and found a terrific apartment in a new housing development near Colgate University, where Steve would be starting his senior year in the fall. I stirred with excitement at the thought of living on my own for the first time in my life. I was actually more excited about that than about being married.

As I walked down the aisle on my father's arm I sensed that something in my relationship was missing. I didn't know what it was, and yet I longed for it. Still, Steve was the best thing in my life and I could not bear to be without him. This did seem to be the right move.

Whether my sister's marriage had been the best move for her was becoming questionable. It was all too apparent with me on my feet, that Barry and Sondra had little in common. As if they had been woven together for the sole purpose of seeing me well, they began to drift apart. Sondra grew more dissatisfied as time passed and she sensed the huge gulf between them. They were eventually divorced, and as I look back I can only feel tremendous gratitude toward both of them, for it was I who benefited most from their union.

My fall at Colgate University was deliriously happy. I was surrounded by people my own age, as our building housed mostly Colgate students. We became very friendly with three fellows who lived diagonally across the hall, and there were always parties or small get-togethers taking place. While some of us played guitars and sang, others watched ball games and played chess. Most everyone smoked pot. I found myself being drawn into spiritual discussions with my friends.

People were getting interested in Baba Ram Dass and tapes of him speaking were circulating around campus. He spoke of meditation and of the peace of mind that could be achieved through giving up the ego. This idea appealed to me because my ego was so deflated as a result of my ileostomy. I found it comforting to explore the spiritual rather than the physical plane, where, in my mind, I no longer made the grade.

I figured that in the spring or summer I would probably have surgery to reconnect by bowel, but I kept pushing the event into the future now, afraid to rock the boat. Little did I know that the boat was about to start rocking anyway.

Chapter Three

My Second Illness

By the end of November the party came to an end. Toward the middle of the month I began to feel extremely weak, so much so that I couldn't ignore it. I soon felt mildly ill and experienced headaches. Before long it was overwhelming.

Steve and I were planning to come home for Thanksgiving break and so my mother made an appointment with -- guess who -- good old Dr. Marvin. After all this time, he had taken over my case again. Unfortunately, it seemed as though we would be needing his services again.

I couldn't believe how disillusioning it felt to be back in the doctor's office. It didn't seem possible that I could actually be ill again. Dr. Marvin was very sympathetic as he drew blood from my arm. He assured us that he would call as soon as he had some results.

When the doctor did call, he spoke to my mother. It appeared that I had hepatitis, but the doctor said that he did not see this as something to be overly concerned about. He explained that with proper bed rest and care the liver usually repairs itself. I was instructed to have monthly blood tests. The doctor felt that within six months' time I would probably be well.

There was no prescribed treatment beyond bed rest, but then nothing seemed more disturbing to me than the idea of being back in bed again. To make matters even worse, Steve made me promise to give up marijuana. We both felt guilty about it possibly playing a role in making me ill, and so I reluctantly agreed.

Of course my parents wanted me to convalesce at home, but I insisted upon returning with Steve to Colgate. I wasn't ready to surrender my newfound freedom. As the dishes and garbage piled up, however, I grew sadder and lonelier. All of my friends, busy and actively involved in their lives, only served to remind me of how pathetic my situation was. As I saw it, I was already badly disfigured by my ileostomy. It was unbelievable to me that I could actually be incapacitated again, this time by a sick liver. The cloud of illness that engulfed me never seemed to end. I began to agree with my parents that I might be better off at home.

I went back and forth between Colgate and home throughout the rest of the school year. I was frustrated, stopped in my tracks. I had just begun to spread my wings when I was forced to return to the nest again.

I had regular blood tests, always expecting to see change for the better, but as winter turned to spring we saw no improvement at all. Dr. Marvin grew concerned as the disease was not behaving as he had expected it to. He informed my parents that he was afraid that I might have the chronic form of hepatitis, which grows progressively worse. He insisted that I see a doctor, an associate of his in Manhattan, who specialized in liver illness.

A liver biopsy was done sometime in May. I was very frightened, as always, by the medical procedure. I found myself shaking as the specialist, after anesthetizing my right side with Novocaine, somehow managed to extract a piece of liver through my skin. Like a scene from an old movie played over and over, my sister and mother rushed to my bedside to comfort me. None of us could believe the endlessness of this tunnel. The doctor said we would have the results in about a week, and that until then he could tell us nothing.

During this time my mother gave me a copy of The Search for Bridey Murphy in the hope of taking my mind off things. It was about a woman who under hypnosis remembered an existence in another lifetime. I was completely fascinated by the concept and through the book was introduced to the gifted psychic, Edgar

Cayce. I quickly purchased a few of his books and found myself enthralled and excited by what I read.

Cayce, who had never read any book in his life except the Bible, could go into a trance state in which he would speak fluently in medical terms. He would make diagnoses and prescribe cures. Known as the "Sleeping Prophet," he was sometimes called in on medical cases when doctors were unable to determine the cause of a given problem. He even delved into the past lives of his patients, clarifying their present situation through his perceptions of their past.

I was deep into Cayce when the biopsy results came back. They showed conclusively that I had the chronic form of hepatitis, which was all the more dangerous, my doctors explained, because they couldn't operate on the liver. Unlike my last disease when we had been able to cut away diseased portions of my intestines, we were now powerless. The doctors saw no way to stop this disease from consuming my liver. They did not tell me, but my parents understood, that this could be fatal.

I didn't fully comprehend the seriousness of what was happening. Both doctors agreed that I should start taking cortisone again, in the hope that the drug would slow down the progress of the disease. With time they hoped, researchers might discover a cure. Dr. Marvin encouraged us to give money to research while the specialist insisted on my doing some daily exercise so as not to lose muscle tone. They both clearly explained that the cortisone could not cure my disease but might possibly retard its growth.

My parents felt desperate. My father hired a young medical student to research my disease to see if there were any developments that my doctors were not aware of. I, not knowing the extent of my problem, didn't take it too seriously and kept reading about Edgar Cayce.

One case history really moved me. Cayce had been called in on a case by the parents of a young girl declared insane by her doctors. When the doctors suggested that she be committed to a sanitarium, her parents, unwilling to accept this fate, contacted Cayce. From a trance state Cayce described the girl's problem. He claimed that she had a wisdom tooth impinging on a nerve; if the tooth was extracted, the girl would return to normal. The result showed that he was correct. The wisdom tooth was removed and the girl resumed normal life.

My first reaction after reading this was to feel sorry for myself that Edgar Cayce was no longer alive and couldn't be brought in to consult on my case. Then, a few nights later while milling all of this around in my mind, I discovered Steve looking despondent. It wasn't like him to be down. "They have nothing to help you with," he said. "This time it's really bad and your parents aren't telling you everything. I'm really worried," he said. "You have to do something! This thing is fatal. Don't you understand? You have to do something!" For the first time the full realization of what was happening hit me. I knew that Steve was right. I couldn't just sit back and accept this fate. If there was a way out of sickness, I had to find it, no matter where it led me.

My mind began to race as I analyzed all the material I had been reading. I reasoned that Cayce saw the wisdom tooth pressing on the nerve in the girl's brain. That meant that in the trance state part of Cayce was able to see into the girl's mouth. Part of Cayce must be mobile! His physical body was obviously not mobile while he was sleeping, so there must be a portion of him that was not physical and could see and travel beyond physical barriers. Then, seemingly from out of nowhere, came the memory of Keith Gonsalves telling me about the man in the sanctuary. I reasoned that if Cayce could do what he did, then maybe the stories Keith had told me had a basis in reality. Maybe energy could travel trans-atlantically -- maybe it just could! At this point, with no particular conviction, but with a far more open mind than I had at eighteen, I decided to pursue my father's friend, to search for the man in the sanctuary.

Chapter Four

The Commencement of Healing
My Miraculous Recovery

Fortunately we were able to contact Keith right away. He researched the matter and told us the man's name was Harry Edwards, and his sanctuary was located in Guilford, Surrey, England.

My father, who had an office in London at the time, asked one of his secretaries to call the sanctuary. We were told that I should write a letter to Mr. Edwards stating my name, address, age, and problem. It was not necessary for me to go into great detail about my illness, but I should be sure to give the name of any diagnosis made, and to make mention of whatever symptoms I was suffering from. I remember thinking that it couldn't be possible that a mere letter was all that was required of me. No one was asking me to take off my clothes, have my blood tested, or even take an X ray. Surely if this could work, it was the kindest thing, but how could it work? As I sat on my parents' poolside patio to write what became a ten-page letter, I was curious and hopeful, but quite skeptical at the same time.

My father was scheduled to make a trip to London at the end of the week. Although he didn't believe in spiritual healing, he offered to take the letter to Mr. Edwards himself.

My father saw Mr. Edwards on the morning of June 17, 1971. That evening, prior to his return, I had so much energy that I was flying! I remember that night so clearly.

I went with Steve to his parents' home. For the first time in six months I didn't feel the need to drop into the first available chair. Instead I walked around, telling everyone how much better I was feeling. What was even more intriguing was the sensation of pins and needles on my right side, within and surrounding the area where the biopsy had been done. I felt certain that something was happening, for I clearly felt more energy than I had known in six months. I had a sense of well-being as if I were (in the words Harry Edwards often used to describe it) "on top of the world."

Steve's family and my own noticed my exuberance and were glad. They found it hard, though, to accept my opinion that something was happening and looked for "rational" explanations for the way I was feeling. I, on the other hand, was excited. I knew what I was feeling, and I knew what it felt like to be weak all the time. There was the tingling sensation to consider, also. Up until then I had had no sensation in my liver. It wasn't until the biopsy was done that I had any real idea of where the liver was even located. Now I was feeling it tingle with energy. I remembered what Keith had told me about his friends in the Bahamas, and how they experienced a tingling sensation in their bodies before their arthritis cleared up.

When my father returned a day later, he handed me two books that Harry had given him and said, "Well, he looks like an ordinary guy to me." I began reading immediately, devouring every word, trying to understand what healing was about and what had happened to me the other night. Surely I could not forget the feeling of energy that pervaded my being! Although the next day the tingling had ceased, and I was not experiencing that same high level of energy, I felt substantially better that I had been feeling.

About five days later I received my first letter from Harry Edwards. I have saved it all these years. It is dated June 17, 1971.

Dear Sheri Perl,

I have seen your father this morning and he has given me your letter. I am placing you within my immediate healing intercessions as from today, primarily in the first instance, to give you new strength and vitality to build up your general health, tone, and resistance. This will enable the healing to overcome the hepatitis condition--which, being a functional disorder, will need some time to be adjusted and overcome the weakness.

Your letter is very clear and the detail you provide gives me a very clear picture of your trouble.

Furthermore, the talk I had with your father this morning, also has given me a still clearer picture of yourself; and this is so helpful to enable our intercessions to be directive and have purpose.

While it is not within my province, to give you any undertaking or promise in advance, I shall not fail to seek help to reach you in every way which can possibly be.

At the outset, I would like you to write to me weekly, giving me just a brief report of your condition, whether you are feeling stronger, happier, better, with less pain, and easier function--or not--just as it is.

I am enclosing my Notes of Absent Healing. I have given your father a copy of these; in order to explain a little about what "absent healing" entails.

I am also posting to you by sea mail a copy of our Spiritual Healer magazine, for your interest.

Looking forward to the future, and having some good news from you,

I am Yours sincerely,

Harry Edwards

I read the letter many times, going over and over his words in my mind. He could offer me no promise in advance but he would not fail to seek help for me. It seemed so mysterious. What kind of help did he mean, and how could it find me? If it hadn't been for the improvement I was experiencing, I might think he was deluded. It really did seem, though, that something very powerful was affecting me. Something I certainly couldn't see, feel, or touch.

Two weeks after the day my father met Harry, I had my usual monthly set of blood tests. Dr. Marvin said that they were "dramatically improved." They had moved one third of the way toward normal. The doctor sounded surprised. I was ecstatic. I immediately sent off a letter to Harry to tell him the good news and became more seriously involved with my reading.

I should mention here that I was still taking cortisone because I was afraid to diverge from my doctor's orders. Although there are those who say that healing cannot take place as long as one takes medical drugs, Harry never asked me to change the medical course I was on.

I grew more and more fascinated with healing. To me it seemed as if magic was becoming real, or perhaps what I thought of as magic wasn't really magic at all, but rather forces and energies I didn't understand.

According to Harry, he was working in conjunction with what he referred to as "spirit doctors." He explained that when a person died his or her spirit would continue to live on in a spirit world in which there are many options for action. The spirits who take pleasure in helping to heal the sick on the earth plane are the ones he referred to as spirit doctors. Harry believed that during a period of meditation (which he referred to as his intercessions) that he would reach a state of attunement in which he could communicate with the spirit doctors. He would inform the spirit doctors of who needed healing, where they lived, and what the trouble seemed to be. He felt that the remainder of the healing was carried out by the spirit doctors.

Because there is no physical distance in the spirit world, a spirit can be anywhere on earth in no time. Harry taught that in many cases the spirit doctors would approach their patients while they were sleeping and their minds were more open. The spirit doctors would then direct energy to the portion of the body that was sick. They would also look beyond the physical symptom to its cause.

Harry contended that all illness has a psychosomatic origin. This does not mean that the illness is not real, but that its cause stems from within the patient's mind and emotions. Harry explained that the spirit doctors would work to soothe the emotional strain that was giving rise to the type of energy that triggered the physical breakdown. Harry felt that frustration, disappointment, nervousness or sadness could easily impair the functioning of the body. Therefore, Harry explained, when healing energy is directed to the dis-ease that is underlying the disease, the potential exists to cure anything, even diseases considered medically incurable.

It all sounded unbelievable, but I couldn't deny the marvelous improvement in my health. I began looking behind and within things for the evidence of spirit life, disappointed that I could not see even one apparition. If spirits were trying to help me, I wanted to see them. At the time I didn't understand that it is not likely to see spirit through physical eyes, and that I was far too frightened to allow my perceptions to open up on other levels.

I began to live and to breathe and to talk healing. I was so amazed by what was happening to me that I couldn't contain my excitement. I spoke to anyone who would listen. Friends with a mere common cold received the entire rundown. I had hoped to find someone who shared my enthusiasm. Reluctantly I came to see that the people I knew in 1971 weren't even remotely ready to open their minds to the idea of an unseen reality that existed in cooperation with our own. To my own mind it did not sound particularly rational either, yet beyond rationality I had my experience to consider. My experience and senses told me that something miraculous was taking place. The phenomenon of spiritual healing was still confusing to me, but its effects were not. I felt better than I had felt in a very long time. I was encouraged and hopeful that the healing would continue to reach me until I could clearly say that I was a hundred percent well again!

In the fall of 1971 Steve and I moved to Cambridge, MA, where he would be attending Harvard Business School. We found a wonderful furnished apartment with a big sunny kitchen just a short distance from school. I enrolled in the Cambridge Center for Adult Education, signing up for courses in jewelry making and Yoga breathing. I hoped that my health would continue to improve and then everything would be okay.

In September I had another set of blood tests. Dr. Marvin again reported dramatic improvement. The tests had now moved about two-thirds of the way toward normal. I was on my way, as far as I was concerned, and nothing could stop me now.

I wrote to Harry about twice a month, for myself as well as for others. I began to make an experiment of writing for people who were in difficulty and observing the results of Harry's efforts. In some cases I observed undeniably positive results, while in others I wasn't sure. I began to wonder why some people responded to Harry's efforts, as I did, with a rapid and powerful reaction, while others did not seem to be touched. Why would what worked so beautifully for me not necessarily work for another? I had read that sometimes a patient isn't "open" to the healing, but at the time I couldn't understand what that meant. "Certainly," I thought, "everyone wants to get well." It made no sense to me to assume that someone might be blocking the healing somehow, and so the question remained unsolved for me for quite a few years.

Probably the most valuable thing I derived from the fall in Cambridge was what I learned in my Yoga breathing class. I had never realized how shallow my breathing was, nor had it ever occurred to me that the cells of my body just might need more oxygen than they were getting. Harry had sent me information on what he called "Characterized Breathing" (you will learn to use this in my healing program that follows), a deep-breathing process that he felt allowed a person to absorb cosmic energy from the atmosphere. Although I tried to use it, until I took the Yoga breathing classes my habitual breathing patterns were too shallow for it to work. Now for the first time in my life I was learning to exhale deeply, completely emptying my lungs, which allowed for a far greater intake of oxygen than my body had ever known. Somehow my mind drew the analogy that now I was breathing an entire sentence, where before I was only breathing a few words. Shortly after this new breathing became habitual, I found that at about three or four P.M. each day I would feel out of breath and would retire to my bed and work on my breathing. It was as if the beginning of proper breathing made apparent to me how starved I had been for breath. As the winter approached, I was feeling stronger and more convinced that spiritual healing was a real phenomenon, despite anyone else's disbelief in it, or in me.

As December rolled around it was arranged for me to have another set of blood tests done by the liver specialist who had done the biopsy. I remember being very annoyed that he would not allow Steve to remain in the room with me, (he was now my husband) while he examined me in front of a crew of interns. At least examinations for liver problems are not as embarrassing as examinations for bowel problems.

I told the doctor that I felt I was getting better. He told me not to get my hopes up, because my disease was not curable. The cortisone I was taking could give me a false impression of having energy. I didn't dare tell him about Harry Edwards and the spirit doctors; however, I did tell him a little about the natural foods I was eating. He replied that I should be careful that I didn't turn orange from drinking too much carrot juice. It was apparent that he wasn't too impressed with my ideas and so I quickly curtailed the conversation, gave him his five vials of blood, and split. The results would be back in a week. I would call him then.

I was very anxious about the tests. If everything was proceeding as I hoped it was, then I should be pretty near normal. I wanted to be well desperately but along with that, there was even more than my health at stake. Not only did I want to be well for the sake of finally being well, but I was now beginning to believe in an unseen world, and I couldn't bear to have that vision shattered. All of a sudden life had become full of magical possibilities that I did not want to lose.

I was so nervous on the Friday afternoon that I was due to call the doctor that Steve made the call for me. As he held the phone to his ear, I searched his face for a sign. When he grinned and put his thumbs up, I grabbed the phone. "Count your blessings," the doctor said. "It's really a miracle. Your tests are practically normal. It looks like the cortisone did the trick!" "The cortisone, my ass," I thought as I thanked him and put down the receiver.

That night I sat down to write to Harry. I had not yet completed my letter when, the next day, the following letter from Harry was in my mailbox. It was dated December 1971 and it read as follows:

Dear Friend,

I feel that the healing has finally reached you. This week you will be having tests and those tests will prove to you the good news that healing has taken place.

When you receive this news, please write to me so that we may all confirm the good news that healing has taken place.

With best wishes,
Yours Sincerely,

Harry Edwards

You can imagine my elation. As far as I was concerned, I now had conclusive proof that Harry and I were involved in some kind of paranormal communication. He not only knew about the tests without me (or anyone else) telling him, but he knew that the results were positive before I did. Surely on some metaphysical plane, it was established that I was well, and Harry could see that. I jumped up and down for joy! No one was going to tell me that it was all in my head again--or at least I wasn't going to feel threatened if they did!

On Monday I called back the specialist to tell him that I knew that I was well, and that I wanted to start weaning off the cortisone right away. It had severe side effects, and I was particularly bothered by mood swings and depression. His reaction was as follows: "Young lady, if you get off the cortisone there is a fifty-fifty chance you will relapse, and if you relapse, an eighty percent chance that you will die! Do not stop taking your medication!"

He was quite clear, and I knew, as I hung up the phone, that I had an important decision to make. "He knows nothing of spiritual healing," I reasoned, "so how can I let him be the authority?" My decision was made. I was going to get off the drug.

I knew that my parents could not bear the knowledge of what I was going to do, so I kept it a secret from everyone but Steve.

This worked out beautifully. Steve had dropped out of school. We were both feeling disillusioned with the established world. My father had arranged for us to live and work in Utah, on a horse ranch owned by one of his friends. The plan was for Steve to work closely with the trainer of the ranch and learn as much as he could about the quarter-horse business. Eventually we would establish our own ranch in New York State, with my father as our partner.

What this meant for the present was that Steve and I were going to purchase a travel trailer, stock it with whatever we needed, and head west to St. George, Utah. As I look back, I really have to thank my father for arranging this situation for me;

it was certainly what I needed most, at this point in my recovery.

First of all, the physical separation from my family was necessary in order for me to get off cortisone. Because the withdrawal process from cortisone induces noticeable weakness, I would never be able to hide what I was doing from my parents. I knew that I could not handle their fears on top of my own.

Second, I was relieving myself of enormous mental and social pressures. If I was going to live on a ranch, I wouldn't have to burden myself with thoughts about whether I should be in college. I could let go of my concerns regarding my appearance or sense of style. And at the same time, I could forget my ill self. I could now see myself as a well person, and the people around me wouldn't know otherwise. The idea of being on my own again restored my faith that I would indeed have my own life, and be able as well, to live it.

I was relieved the day we finally left, eager to start reducing the drug. From my past experience with cortisone withdrawal, I knew that I was bound to feel very weak physically and emotionally. And because the main symptom of my last disease was weakness, I knew the withdrawal would be all the more frightening. I wouldn't know until the entire ordeal was over whether the weakness I experienced was a result of the withdrawal process or an indication of a relapse.

It's a good thing that I was prepared for a tumultuous time, for most assuredly, I had one. It doesn't sound like it would produce such dramatic results. I merely took five and a half pills instead of six upon arising and repeated that dosage twice a day. By that evening, however, I felt exhausted, and I was worried and upset. My fears had a field day. Maybe I had done the wrong thing, maybe I was really deluded. Maybe all this Harry Edwards business was in my mind and now I would relapse and die.

I then reminded myself that I was going through withdrawal and would naturally assume the worst. Usually at this point I would reread Harry's letters, focusing on the one in which he said

I would be having tests soon, and that the tests would prove that healing had taken place. I tried to assure myself that this was real! I obviously didn't really understand or know if I fully believed in spiritual healing, but I knew what had taken place. I was over the disease, and just going through cortisone withdrawal. I spent many a night reading through Harry's letters, assuring myself that, in fact, I was well, and had not harmed myself by reducing the drug.

The withdrawal period usually lasted two or three days, during which time I felt terribly weak and ill at ease. Then my body would adjust to the present dosage and I would feel normal again. I would then wait about a week before reducing the drug again, so that I could prolong my experience of having energy, in this way reassuring myself that I could safely continue on this course. When I felt sufficiently confident, I would eliminate another half pill and begin the process all over again.

From my understanding of it, cortisone is normally produced in the adrenal glands and is, in actuality, a form of adrenaline, which supplies the body with energy. When cortisone is taken in large amounts, the adrenal glands register so much extra adrenaline in the body that they no longer work to produce it, and can shrink to the size of a pea. They can regenerate (thank goodness), but before they do, they have to experience the lack of cortisone in the body, and then respond to it, by producing the necessary adrenaline. That time of deficiency is the hard part.

Things were worst when I reduced the dosage from one pill to a half. We were already in Utah now, becoming close friends with Max, the horse trainer, and his wonderful family. No one could understand why I had become so quiet and withdrawn. I spent evenings in the trailer rereading Harry's letters, trying to assure myself that the severe weakness and depression would pass. When I finally adjusted to the half pill, I felt great and decided to give myself a few weeks' rest before taking the last and final plunge.

Originally I had planned to keep all of this secret from my parents until I was off the drug completely for at least two weeks, but in my elation I let it slip out. During a phone conversation, my mother asked if I needed my prescription refilled. Unable to resist, I said, "I don't need any more of the crap!"

"What did you say?" she inquired.

I boasted proudly, "I've been on a half a pill for three weeks and I feel great. Tomorrow I go to zero!"

My mother didn't know how to react. She was delighted and worried at the same time. To think that I was off the drug and feeling well was a miracle, but was it safe to be off the drug? She felt somewhat reassured to know that this had been going on for close to three months now, that I had gone through major withdrawals and had come through them feeling well. And I think she was glad that I hadn't told her earlier.

When I dropped the last half pill from my life, I expected a fairly rough time. I was thrilled to discover that I felt nothing at all. I guess the dosage, so minimal at this point, was not enough to be missed. After three days with no reaction I knew that I had been freed of affliction. I wasn't fully convinced that I understood how, but I was desperate to learn and to somehow become involved in spiritual healing. For the first time in many years, I felt truly well. I used to take long walks around the ranch, crying with joy, from the simple feeling of nothing being wrong.

Now that I was off all medication, I decided that I would never have anything to do with medical doctors again, if I could help it. I knew that this meant that I would never have the opportunity to reverse the ileostomy, but at this time, I couldn't imagine that I would ever be able to make the choice to put myself through surgery. I was so grateful to be alive and well that I figured the ileostomy was one cross I would have to bear.

I was full of wonder and gratitude, gratitude at being alive, and wonder at the forces that enabled me to be so.

Chapter Five

My First Conclusions Regarding My Healing

Meeting Harry Edwards
All Roads Point to Meditation

As a result of my astonishing recovery and the means through which it came about, I was drawn to study the inner world and the powers and forces within. After all, my body had become well very quickly in what seemed to me direct response to the efforts of Harry Edwards in England. Somehow he had reached me, and had done so through a means that was obviously not physical. No physical contact was made, no physical medicine was taken, nothing in the outside physical world had changed, and yet the most dramatic changes had taken place in my body.

As I began to sort out the events as I saw them, certain conclusions came to mind: Harry, through thought or meditation or -- in his words – attunement with the spirit doctors, was able to direct energy to me. In response to this energy, illness in my body was overcome.

Because I could not see, feel, hear, touch, or taste this energy, I concluded that the energy was not physical. Because its effects were quite physical, I could not deny its presence. I therefore concluded that energy, not perceivable to the average human being exists, similar to the way that television and radio waves exist in the atmosphere. I began to think of this energy as spiritual waves; henceforth I could now accept the term spiritual energy, for it meant just that: energy that existed, but not in physical form.

Because physical form can be so drastically affected by this energy, it is obviously receptive to it. Because it is receptive to it, there must be a counterpart within the physical system that allows for this to be received and integrated. Since we do not know of any part of the physical body that allows for the acceptance of spiritual energy, the receptacle of this energy must be nonphysical itself, or spirit. I now could accept that I must be in part spirit; and that all beings must be in part spirit. Somehow the spiritual essence of all life must be embedded in it from the start, but I had never bothered to think about it, and had always assumed that what I saw was all that existed. I now began to think that what I saw was just the tip of the iceberg; the outermost covering to a much greater reality of spirit, which interpenetrated all that I saw. Not only did it interpenetrate it, but in actuality it might just govern it, for the spiritual energy was able to heal from the inside that which was not considered healable from the outside.

It began to seem to me that life worked from the inside out, and that many forces that we might not be in touch with could have a controlling effect on our lives. If this was true, it seemed clear to me that I had better try to learn what those forces were and how they worked in me, or I might just end up ill again. Therefore, I consciously began my quest for a greater understanding of what seemed to me a very mysterious spirit world.

I spent a lot of time reading books about healing. I was fascinated with the concept of a spirit reality that not only existed but worked in cooperation with our own. I wanted to be in touch with this reality, and longed for experiences that would prove to me even more conclusively that spirit existence was real. Despite my experience, I still had my doubts, which I desired to eliminate.

To this end I organized all sorts of spiritual meetings, holding seances (unsuccessfully, I might add) with anyone who would take part, including many of the ranch hands, who neither believed nor cared for any of my ideas. I tried to develop my own healing abilities by working on the ill animals at the ranch, placing my hands on them and imagining that healing energy was entering into them. You could say that my focus was turned inward, as I tried to experience and understand the spiritual nature of life, but at the same time I was learning an enormous amount about living on the land: cooking, sewing, and tending to animals. As Steve worked with Max, the horse trainer of the ranch, I had the opportunity to spend a good deal of time with his wife. I grew to love Yvonne, and their seven children, feeling a part of their healthy, loving, strong, hardworking family. My environment was challenging without being at all threatening.

After a year in the west, Steve and I drove our travel trailer to upstate New York, where we searched for and found our farm. I had a very strong feeling about one particular farm, and felt that it was meant to be ours. I also sensed that when we finally settled onto it, I would find a teacher who would teach me what I was seeking to know.

Prior to settling on our farm, Steve and I made a trip to England to meet Harry Edwards, something that was very important to me. We both knew that once we began to work our farm, we would be responsible for the lives of many animals and would not be able to get away so easily.

I found Harry to be the same down-to-earth, kind, and good-natured man that he was in his letters. In his simple and easy manner, he showed us around the beautiful grounds and gardens of Burrows Lea, and then he took us inside to join in a healing session. I anticipated feeling something momentous, and was disappointed not to feel intense heat or energy emanating from his hands. I was still looking for tangible proof that spirit reality was real and that I had not imagined the whole thing.

While roaming the grounds around the sanctuary, we met a young man from Ireland who said that he was a medium. Peter was very helpful to me and satisfied some of my curiosity about the spiritual plane. He invited us to his hotel where he played a recording made at a Leslie Flint séance, and I was riveted! Now, for the first time I heard spirits speaking on tape. I couldn't get enough. We spoke much over the next several days.

Before we parted, Peter gave me a list of British books he thought would be helpful to me. Among them were books by White Eagle, a spirit communicator who spoke through a medium by the name of Grace Cooke. The material was fascinating to me, and I was finding the spiritual books more important and interesting than the psychology books that had been my fancy a few years before.

I liked White Eagle immediately. I felt that he was a very loving spirit and his writings further confirmed my views that realities, beyond those we can see, feel, and touch, do indeed exist. When he spoke of healing, he expressed the need for meditation as a way of tuning yourself into a higher vibration. I remembered that Harry had said that it was necessary for him to reach a state of attunement in order to make contact with the spirit doctors. As I thought about it, I began to realize that practically everything I had read concerning healing mentioned the importance of meditation.

I decided that the time had come for me to learn to meditate. Not knowing how else to begin, I drove into town from the farm one day and purchased a number of books. None were all that helpful because reading about meditation didn't exactly help me learn how to do it. I understood in theory that meditation involved focusing on one thought, word, or image in order to slow down the thoughts rushing through your mind. In practice, I had no idea where to begin.

I was considering Transcendental Meditation when a friend of mine who had recently completed TM came to the farm. I told her of my desire to meditate and she offered to teach what she knew. She also chose a mantra for me.

Cynthia explained that in Transcendental Meditation you are given a mantra by your instructor. A mantra is a word or sound that you repeat over and over again in your head, focusing your attention upon it and away from your usual thoughts. Cynthia chose for me the word sohom, which I liked a lot. Together we set up a special room in the upstairs of my home to be used as a meditation room.

We cut fresh flowers and placed them around the room, lit candles, and set incense to burn (something I still love to do) before we sat down to meditate. I don't know exactly what I expected, but I was definitely disappointed. I said the word sohom over and over in my mind but it seemed impossible to keep my mind from wandering. I had remembered reading that it was natural for the mind to wander. It was advised that in that situation one should, without getting upset, take notice of the wandering mind, and then center oneself again on their mantra. I tried but I couldn't help getting upset, and when I resumed focusing on my mantra, I didn't feel centered. I just felt frustrated! I would get bored repeating this monotonous word and my mind would naturally find something else to do. I had hoped to reach "attunement" and meet my spirit guides, and all I was doing was day-dreaming. Some meditation that was! But I figured that I would have to keep trying a little longer before forming an opinion, because everything I read kept pointing me to meditation.

As a result of my interest in meditation, I began reading books about Eastern philosophy. Again I was exposed to the idea of transcending the ego through meditation. I found myself intrigued by this idea because it seemed that my life would be less difficult if I wasn't suffering so much from my now deflated ego. I reasoned that the sadness surrounding my ileostomy would be lessened if my ego wasn't so powerful. It also seemed that it might be easier to maintain a state of positive thinking (something Harry Edwards and White Eagle felt extremely necessary) if I had less of an ego to satisfy. Wasn't it my ego that found fault with my life and with myself? I also understood through my reading that when a person truly transcended their ego, that they were then able to fully merge with the greater forces of the universe, enabling them to become a more powerful person, or even a healer. All of this appealed to me. I committed myself to daily meditation to see what would develop.

Ever since living with the ileostomy I had taken a bath each morning in order to totally remove the appliance from my body and cleanse myself in the warm, comforting water. During this time I would dilate the stoma, as I still had the constriction problem. Because this usually took about thirty minutes, I decided to meditate while soaking in the tub so as not to take any longer getting my day started.

What began as a matter of practicality became a matter of practice when I discovered that meditation and bathing worked extremely well together. The warm water helped to induce relaxation, and being in the bath removed me from the rest of my home and activities.

Every morning I would immerse myself in a warm tub, make myself as comfortable as possible, dilate the stoma, and begin to repeat the sound sohom. For the longest time I felt as though nothing of value was taking place, however, after a number of weeks I began to notice how much deeper my breathing had become, and how relaxed my arms and legs were. Even though my breathing technique was constantly interrupted by my thinking mind, my continual effort to return to breath was taking some of the wind out of my sails and I could feel the relaxation that resulted from breaking the momentum of my thoughts by returning to the breath. Sometime after that, while concentrating on the sound sohom, I began to hear my own breath as it went in and out of my nostrils. As I listened further, the sound of my breath seemed to make the sound sohom. It sounded to me as if my breath made the sound "so" as I inhaled and made the sound "hom" as I exhaled. In time I stopped using the mantra and simply listened to the sound of my breath entering and leaving me.

Although I had not found a way to silence my mind, practicing this breathing technique helped me to take a step back, behind all those thoughts that usually monopolized my attention. This provided a short respite for me, and I could feel, that when I stepped back from my thoughts for even a second, that I relaxed substantially.

Working with this breathing meditation also allowed me to witness my own thoughts, which was a new experience for me. In the past, I would have a thought and then I would react to it. Now, while practicing meditation, I would have the thought, realize that I had lost my focus on breath, and then while returning to the breath I would see the thought from a distance, so to speak.

This was enlightening, because I was getting a bird's eye view of my own thinking mind which I had never seen so clearly before. In some ways it was a humbling process because I became aware of all the crazy thoughts that went through my mind on any given day. For the first time I clearly saw that I was way too hard on myself and overly judgmental, especially of myself. I saw that I was fearful of a great many things and even though I was observing and coming to know myself, I was frustrated with the whole process because I didn't see how any of this was going to take me to the "promised land." I wanted to develop as a healer and I longed to grow spiritually, but I couldn't see any of that happening. The books I read spoke of finding peace by transcending the human condition, but I was human and I couldn't, for the life of me, imagine transcending myself! Was it really possible to think only positive thoughts and love everyone unconditionally?

My dream was to travel to England and study with Harry Edwards himself. Of course I knew this wasn't possible, and Harry wasn't teaching any classes for healers anyway. I was thrilled when Harry sent me literature about a correspondence course he was developing to train healers. For the first time in my life I was thoroughly enthusiastic about the idea of being in school. I read the textbooks, studied Harry's theories with zest and determination, and was more than eager to take the written examination that arrived a few months later. I was not surprised when I passed. I was also extremely happy to discover that as a result, I was certified as a member of the National Fellowship of Healing. This certification came through the National Federation of Spiritual Healers, of which Harry was the honorary president.

I also continued my efforts to learn more about meditation and spirituality. I attended classes and consulted with teachers and gurus. Each time I left a session, however, I felt definite disappointment. I was no more enlightened than when I entered the session. My instructors basically confirmed that the technique I was already using was more than adequate.

It was now clear to me that I had no idea of what truth or enlightenment or oneness with the universe meant. They sounded like desirable states but it seemed to me that neither I, nor most of the people who talked about them, really understood what they were talking about. I knew there was something I needed to understand, but I had no real idea of what it was. I continued meditation in the hope that it would help bring me closer to where I wanted to be--although I couldn't define what or where that was. I sensed a feeling of mental freedom inside me that longed to be unleashed. I sensed a state of greater peace of mind inside me that I longed to tap into. I sensed things, but I couldn't put my finger on them. I hoped that meditation would help me to find them.

Then one day I overheard a young woman speaking to another woman at a meditation meeting. The first one asked, "What do you do about desire, when you find yourself overcome by it?" The other answered, "I meditate it away. I meditate on the light and it all disappears. The light dissolves it." "Nonsense," I thought. It was right then and there that something inside of me snapped.

I sensed that there was inherent value in meditating, and I

knew that I would continue to practice it in one form or another. However, I was tired of theories that suggested that I become someone else, someone who was peaceful all the time. Were the full range of human emotions supposed to be squashed down into some blissful benignity that I'll admit sounded lovely, but just might not be real? After all we are human. We are endowed with all kinds of feelings and emotions. We desire our first breath, and so we breathe. We desire to be, and so we live. How could all desire be wrong?

I grew very confused. I wanted to be a healer, but I knew that I could not become all those lily-white things that my books and instructors required. My emotions, my desires, my unique personal self were with me no matter how deeply I explored meditation. I felt that I could not give myself up in order to find a deeper self. I realized that my longing to be a healer sprang from my desire to help others, not an emotion that one would want to squelch.

I began trying to separate the contents of the meditation package. I wanted to continue to meditate for many reasons, but not to try to become someone else. I was beginning to realize, however, that I could use meditation to train myself to step back behind my thoughts in order gain some clarity about them, and this proved very valuable, so I kept up with it. Then one day as I was going back to my breath, I realized that I was not any of these thoughts that were running through my mind, but the awareness in which they all took place.

Now that was a break through, because I began to see that even if these thoughts had been running through my mind habitually for most of my life, that they were not me! I felt that it was helpful that meditation allowed me to both observe and step back from fearful and negative thoughts, however, I wondered why I thought this way in the first place, and how I would ever change my way of thinking.

During meditation, many negative, fearful and unhappy

thoughts came up, thoughts I seemed to have very little control over. I became aware of ingrained patterns of thinking. Fearful thoughts, angry thoughts, and stress-provoking thoughts had become habits of a lifetime.

Although meditation helped me to relax because it provided some space between me and my thoughts, it did not help me to change them. I realized that my fears and negative thoughts blocked me from the peace of mind I so desperately wanted. How, I wondered, can I change my way of thinking?

I was longing for help and direction on that fateful day when I discovered the teacher who would finally help me sort some of this out. The person whose presence I sensed when Steve and I first came to purchase our farm was about to enter my life.

Chapter Six

Enter Seth and the Discovery of My Personal Beliefs:

A Fuller Understanding of the Causes Behind My Illness

I first learned of Jane Roberts through one of my sister's friends. Alfredo, who was deeply involved with Jane's work, insisted that Sondra tell me about an incredible medium who lived in the town of Elmira, a twenty-five minute car ride from my farm. This medium, he claimed, was responsible for bringing through a personality of great wisdom. This personality, called Seth, was writing books through Jane--books that were changing the lives of many people.

I was immediately drawn to Jane and Seth. I wasted no time in heading for the Elmira bookstore to purchase all of the Seth books available.

Fortunately the man in the bookstore seemed to have a good deal of practical information concerning Jane. He looked her number up in the telephone book for me and told me that she was listed under her husband's name, Butts. That explained why I couldn't find a number for any Jane Roberts in Elmira. He also informed me that she held weekly ESP classes in her home, the very idea of which sent waves of excitement throughout my body. "Maybe this is it," I thought. "Maybe I'm about to become involved with the teacher I've been waiting for all along."

As I drove back to the farm I planned in my mind how I would call Jane and express to her my need to be a member of her class. I hadn't even read one word in her books, yet I felt a tremendous longing to learn from her.

When Jane answered the phone she sounded warm and friendly. I told her that I had been very interested in spiritual healing and mediumship for a long time. I expressed my strong desire to attend her ESP class. She asked me if I had read any of her books. I told her that I had just purchased a few of them that day. She explained to me that the prerequisite for joining her class was to read The Seth Material and Seth Speaks. At the same time both books were sitting in my lap. If I could have gobbled them up that instant, I would have. Instead I promised her that I would start reading immediately. Jane told me to call her again once I had completed the books.

Now I have never been a fast reader and those of you who have read Seth know that the material isn't particularly fast reading. I was working my way through the books when I felt that I could stand it no longer. I called Jane again approximately one month later. When asked if I had finished the books I told Jane "not completely." I crossed my fingers and made a silent wish. Jane hesitated a moment and then graciously said that I could attend the next class.

My excitement was enormous. I had read in the books that Seth came through Jane during the ESP classes and actually talked to the students. I have to admit that I was terrified at the idea of Seth speaking directly to me, but I wanted to experience the phenomenon anyway. So far my experience with mediumship was limited to reading, looking at photographs taken at séances, and listening to tapes. All of this I had found very interesting. I knew, however, that it could not compare to being in the room with a real spirit speaking through a medium. I also had a very strong sense that I would make valuable friends through these classes, friends that would last throughout my life.

Class was always held on Tuesdays at seven p.m. As I entered Jane and Rob's crowded living room I was shocked to see people drinking wine, smoking cigarettes, cracking jokes, and acting, it seemed to me, in a manner that was not very spiritual.

One couch seemed filled with as many people as could fit on it. All the available chairs were taken while people crowded between, in front of, and behind the chairs.

Not knowing anyone and feeling shy, I took a seat on the floor in a corner of the room and watched. Everyone seemed well acquainted; animated conversations sprang up in every direction. Occasionally I noticed another person who, like myself, sat quietly, but for the most part the group was boisterous. The age range varied. I saw many people who looked to be around my age (twenty-two), while the oldest members must have been in their eighties.

I was trying to figure out who was Jane when she took over control of the room, requesting that everyone settle down. Jane began class by asking members about their dreams. I listened, barely comprehending, as the students gladly volunteered information. Jane laughed at some of the remarks that were made and lit herself a cigarette. She was a small, thin woman with dark shoulder-length hair. Her nose was prominent, but what stood out most on her face were her dark, sharp, intelligent, intent eyes. Though small in stature, Jane didn't seem small in any other way. There was power and wit and wisdom behind those eyes. I felt immediate respect for her.

I was involved in listening to conversations going back and forth between Jane and the class members when all of a sudden I heard a loud and powerful voice take over the conversation. All eyes were riveted on Jane as Seth removed her glasses and became the focal point of the room. "Good evening," Seth said, and "good evening" some answered. I felt frozen to my spot on the floor. I was so scared that I couldn't imagine how the class members interacted so casually with Seth. As I looked at Jane and studied her she definitely appeared different: more masculine, stronger, even more powerful. Although I was too overwhelmed to understand Seth's words there was no doubt in my mind of his presence within Jane's body. A different energy emanated from her now.

I was greatly surprised by Seth's entry. I assumed that candle lighting, or light dimming, or meditating on Jane's part would be necessary to bring Seth through. Instead it happened as easily and naturally as switching channels on a television set. It seemed that Seth could come and go at will, responding to the conversations that took place between the students and Jane. His voice was strong and powerful, not weak and otherworldly. He didn't seem the least bit concerned with appearing quiet or dignified, but instead went out of his way to be humorous and jovial. He teased and cajoled, raised his voice and lowered his voice, spoke strongly and emphatically, as well as softly and tenderly. Although I was not concentrating on his words, there was no denying his presence and the impact it was making on me.

I lost track of time. Midway through the evening, Jane called a class break and left the room. "Now what am I going to do?" I wondered. Because Steve and I were beginning to have marital problems, I had attended class alone. I didn't know anyone and felt intimidated by the many outspoken people. Feeling more than a little lost, I walked into the small kitchen of Jane's Water Street apartment and began to pour myself a cup of tea. I felt someone enter behind me and turned to face a tall, dark young man who I had noticed the minute I arrived in Jane's living room. I had been instantly attracted to him, and when he asked me how I was doing I felt a rush of energy between us. I said I was okay; I wondered who he was. I knew no one there who I could ask, and to make matters worse, I was married. Yet I could hardly deny my desire to know him.

Soon class resumed and I kept my eye on that young man throughout the rest of the evening. I noticed that he was glancing back at me from across the crowded room. I didn't talk at all in class except to answer Jane when she asked me what my impression of class was. "Refreshing," I said. "Refreshing to hear so many people speak honestly to each other." It was the only thing I could think of saying. Shortly after, Jane said that class was over. I approached her quickly to thank her for letting me come. Much to my surprise and pleasure, Jane said that I was welcome to attend class regularly. She added that if for some reason I was unable to attend class, I should phone.

While people milled around talking to Jane and to each other, Sue Watkins, a regular member of the class, walked over to the young man that I had my eye on. Sue told him that he reminded her of Kurt Vonnegut. He noticed me watching and we smiled briefly at each other. From that time on, in my mind, he became the Kurt Vonnegut guy. As I drove back to the farm that night, my mind was filled with thoughts of Jane and Seth, the energy of the evening, and the Kurt Vonnegut guy. Although he stopped attending the classes right after I started attending them, and I didn't speak to him again for several years, I thought of him. He symbolized to me the man that I was looking for. When faced with the dissatisfactions of my marriage, I thought of the Kurt Vonnegut guy and wondered if I would ever be given a second chance to fall in love.

When my second Seth class rolled around, Steve said that he wanted to attend with me. Jane said that if I was comfortable with that, it was certainly okay with her. She knew that he hadn't come with me the first time and I had indicated some marital problems. But Steve and I were trying to sweep them under the rug again, not knowing what other course to take.

Sometimes avoidance worked for a while, but eventually the same issues would arise and we would both grow dissatisfied.

In part, we both knew that I felt paralyzed sexually due to my ileostomy. I felt much more comfortable with my clothes on than off. Steve had hoped that time would eventually bring me out of my shell. Instead, I had less and less interest in sex as time went on and more and more interested in spirituality.

I was very confused. I knew that I longed for so many things that were outside of my little world, but I felt that I dare not reach for them. I felt safe and secure with Steve and yet unfulfilled.

At my third Seth class Jane was talking about Harry Edwards

as I entered the room. "I've had an experience with Harry Edwards," I eagerly said. "Tell us about it," Jane responded. Before I knew it, all the eyes in the room were focused on me. I became very nervous. My lips seemed stuck together as I began to explain how Harry Edwards cured me of liver disease. I explained the amazing blood-test results. Before I could finish my story it seemed as if twenty people shouted all at once. "What beliefs did you change? You must have changed some beliefs. What were they?"

I knew I was in trouble now. "Uh, beliefs, I didn't change any," I said. "It just happened."

"Impossible," the crowd shouted. "You had to have changed some beliefs, or it couldn't have happened!"

"My God," I thought, "what is a belief and what are they all talking about?" At that moment I wished I had read the books through.

The class members were waiting for my response, and I felt unable to find one. Jane, who I'm certain noticed my discomfort, explained that sometimes we change beliefs without even realizing it and I was off the hook. I still didn't understand what they were talking about, however, and I decided to be very quiet so as not to make a fool of myself in front of this boisterous and overwhelming group. I also thought it a good idea to start paying attention to what these Seth teachings were all about. I was fascinated with the demonstration of a spirit speaking, but I realized that there was a philosophy here that I had better learn. So I did. Here it is in a nutshell.

According to Seth, we form our own experience. We are responsible for what happens to us. If we are hit by disaster, we did something to bring it about. In other words, we are not victims.

According to Seth our energy goes out from us and shapes the reality that we know. The kind of energy that flows outward from us is a result of our beliefs. Our beliefs are our thoughts backed up by our emotions.

Seth explains that we all have many beliefs, most of which were formed in our childhood. Most importantly, according to Seth, by changing beliefs, you could change anything.

At the time, I bought into this way of thinking lock, stock and barrel. I loved it, because what it said to me was that if I kept all the right beliefs, I could prevent myself from ever becoming ill again. I question that now.

I realize that what I believe affects how I feel and how I perceive reality. I also know that my perceptions color everything that I see. However, at the same time, I believe that the Seth ideas have been vastly oversimplified. I believe that there is more to the "bigger picture" than what we believe and that other factors can and will come into play.

That said, I believe that on a personal level, our beliefs effect us very much. That is why I think it is wise to observe and examine our personal beliefs because each of us runs a constant dialogue in our heads, and those dialogues influence our lives every day.

It's easy to understand how this works on a personal level. For example, if I had bought into the belief that it was absolutely impossible for me to ever become well, I would not have reached out to Harry Edwards in the first place. If you believe that you are not capable of achieving a certain goal, whether that is true or not, you will be thwarted, by yourself, from ever achieving that goal. You won't follow through, or you won't even get started!

As a result of this realization, I took time everyday to sit quietly in meditation. Initially the work was more about observing the kind of thoughts that arose in my mind on a constant basis. I would start by doing my breathing. When I would catch myself lost in thought, I would jot down the thoughts that had come up. This was a very enlightening process because simply by looking objectively at my habitual thought patterns, I saw what many of my beliefs were. After reviewing the thoughts I was jotting down everyday, it became apparent to me, by the kind of things I worried and daydreamed about, that I didn't believe that I was safe or that my being was good.

My first revelation was that I believed that my body was bad and undesirable as a result of the ileostomy. This was nothing new. I was aware of my feelings about my body since the surgery. However, the significant difference was that I now realized that I was holding a belief about my body, a belief that wasn't necessarily true. Maybe my body wasn't so disgusting. It did what everyone else's did, only differently. And then I began to examine further my beliefs about the human body and its biology, discovering the fact that I had never been comfortable with my body and its biological functions.

I can remember how uneasy I felt if I was on a date and had to excuse myself to go to the bathroom. In some mixed-up way I believed that urinating or moving one's bowels was not feminine and felt ashamed of the most necessary of bodily processes. I felt that my breasts should be placed delicately inside lace bras and my vagina neatly hidden away in lace panties. Then they were clean and feminine and pretty. The fact that my body was a part of nature and something that I should honor completely eluded me.

In a regular ESP class, held on December 10, 1974, Seth's speaking about the human biology had a profound effect upon me. I would like to quote a small section from that session here:

"You think that the soul is a white wall with nothing written upon it, and so your idea of sacrilege is to shit upon it, not realizing that the shit and the soul are one, and that the biological is spiritual, and that, again, if you will forgive my homey concept, that flowers grow from the shit of the earth. The true communion is that all things of this earth return to it and are consumed and rise up again in a new life that is never destroyed, never annihilated, though always changing form.

So when you shrink from such words or meanings, why do you shrink? Because you do not trust the biology of your being or the integrity of your soul in flesh. You are people! You are made of the stuff of the earth, and the dust from the stars has formed into the shit that lies in piles - warm piles that come from the animals and the beasts and the warm creatures of the earth, and that shit fertilizes the flowers, and the ground, and is a part of it.

How dare any of you, therefore, set yourselves up against that or in conflict with it?"

Boy oh boy, did that ever hit home! I realized that my disgust for my ileostomy was powered by my disgust for my biological processes. I also realized that as long as I maintained the view that human-body functions were disgusting, I would always be in conflict with my life. I didn't know how to change these beliefs, but I hoped that understanding them as beliefs, as opposed to facts, would make a difference. It did. In a subtle way I felt less bad about my body.

Like magic, once I had become aware of one belief, many more began to reveal themselves to me. Once I came to see that something I had always taken as a fact of reality was merely my perception of it, then everything was up for reevaluation. How much of what I thought was really as it was? How much was a product of my beliefs? Seth was saying that everything I experienced was a product of my beliefs and that no "rock-bed reality" existed. Instead, Seth explained there were many versions and perceptions, all of which would lead me back to my own beliefs. This concept was fascinating and allowed for all kinds of possibilities, but at first I was very shook-up.

I remember walking into writing class (a small group Jane taught during the day, which I joined far more out of a desire to be around Jane than to write) feeling shaky and unsupported. "It's as if my table was all set," I said, "and even if the place settings were not so hot, they were there and they supported me. Now I feel that none of them are real and I therefore have to remove them, and my table is bare, and it's scary!"

"Well," Jane answered. "There is no reason why you should feel that you have to overturn everything. Keep the beliefs that work for you. Discard only those that you want to discard. No one is telling you that you must turn your entire world upside down." But I felt as though my world were turning upside down of its own accord. "None of it is real," I retorted, "so how can I keep it?"

Once this process of examining my beliefs began, I was no longer sure if I truly knew anything. Every opinion that I held (and I held many opinions about everything) now had to be reevaluated. "This is what I believe about this," I would think, "but is it in fact true, or just my perception of it? If it is merely my perception of it, do I want to believe this anymore? Is it productive for me to believe this?" And in this manner I questioned everything.

As this process went on, I began to experience new feelings associated with the issues I was examining. As I realized, for example, that maybe my body was not so terrible and that it was only my beliefs that made me feel so bad, the pain and horror that had been locked deep inside of me rushed to the surface and demanded release. Now, for the first time, I was ready to face that pain.

I remember spending an entire weekend crying. How I longed for my once perfect body and the nonchalance that had accompanied it. I had always taken that totally for granted. My face dripping with tears, the source of which seemed limitless, I agonized over all the jealousy I felt toward other women who still had their bodies intact. And yet I knew this wasn't their fault. I ached for something I knew I didn't have with Steve. I had known it when I walked down the aisle, but I knew it with far more certainty now. I wondered if I would ever feel secure enough to go off on my own. I understood now that my beliefs in my own inadequacy had manipulated me into thinking that marrying Steve would be the answer to my problems. I knew now that that belief was limiting and was causing both Steve and me a lot of pain.

Every time I thought I had finished crying, another image of my body, or a beautiful girl in a bikini, or of the Kurt Vonnegut guy would rush through my mind, bringing with it an onrush of fresh tears. I felt trapped. I knew what I wanted, but I felt it could never happen. I cried for what I desired and believed would always be denied me--a second chance at love and the reconnection of my bowel.

When I emerged from the weekend, I felt better. I knew my problems were not solved, but I felt lighter. I knew that I was not yet ready to make any dramatic changes in my life with Steve, but I felt more optimistic. I had a sense that the future would somehow lend a hand.

Seth class became the most exciting event in my life. My fear of Seth was turning into love and respect as I grew to see that he had no interest in exposing my secrets to the class. What had made me fear him so much was, again, my beliefs. His wisdom and concern for each one of us forced me to confront all the ridiculous things I had projected upon him. For instance, as I saw it, underneath my exterior lived one scared, marred, hurting turkey who really wasn't what she pretended to be. I feared that Seth, seeing through my facade, would expose my secrets. That ridiculous logic was formed in my beliefs. Seth never saw any of us as anything but good and tried to impress upon each of us, time and time again, the basic goodness of what we were. It was through his teachings that I really came to see how little trust and respect and love I had for my own being. In his books and in many of the classes, Seth spoke to us of the worth and imperfect perfection of our beings right now. The following Seth quote, spoken to the students in class one night, had a powerful effect on me.

"And yet a cat is a perfect cat, whether it is flawed or had a broken toe, or whether it can hear or not hear, or whether it is ancient or young. A cat is a perfect cat. Now you can understand that. But in the same way you have a responsibility to be yourselves as a cat has to be itself. To express the joyful creature nature that is your own. And through that expression your spirituality will flower".

As I listened to such statements, I was forced to take a look at myself. I knew that I didn't feel like a perfect cat. I felt marred, and yet I did recognize that when I looked at an animal with a broken leg, it didn't bother me. I just saw an animal with a broken leg, not a lesser creature. I knew now that I had a lot of work to do just to make peace with myself. It seemed like a tremendous job, but at the same time, it seemed like an absolute must to me. It just made no sense to hold so many things against myself. I was encouraged because I began to see through some of my beliefs and realize that they weren't necessarily true. That was a big step forward and I knew that no matter how hard it was to face, if I couldn't find a way to fully accept my body and myself, I'd never be free to live my life.

One thing that I had learned from my closeness to death's door was that no one is given forever to make life work. I wanted my life to work. I didn't really know what that meant, or how I was going to do it, but I sensed that there was happiness inside of me, happiness that I could possibly tap. I felt that if there was a way to change my perception of my body, I would have to find it. And whether that led me to or away from Steve, I would find my way.

How to go about the business of changing beliefs was another matter. Seth had said that some beliefs could change automatically, as a result of recognizing them as beliefs. However, Seth never said that it would always be easy to change all of them. Each of us would have to discover our own ways, working within the laboratories of our own minds. He gave us some very useful exercises in his books, but again stressed the individual nature of any exercise. According to Seth there was no "right" way to do anything. Each of us would have to discover the ways that worked best for ourselves.

I decided that I would just continue on with my daily practice of meditation, adding some "belief work" to the mix.

In many ways we are all like our own hypnotists and our own subjects, hypnotized by our own beliefs. Seth discussed suggestion as one possible way of changing beliefs. When questioned by a student about how to believe in his basic goodness (when he didn't believe that he was good), Seth instructed him to tell himself over and over that he was good until he believed it. Seth said that we should watch the suggestions that we were feeding ourselves, and consciously change our suggestions wherever we found them limiting.

It seemed to me that the process was threefold. Certainly I first had to recognize what my belief was, allowing myself to feel the emotions connected with that belief, and to fully acknowledge its presence in my life. Then I would challenge that belief, just by acknowledging that it was a belief and not necessarily a fact of reality. Lastly, I would start using positive suggestion.

Because I was already working with meditation and deep breathing every morning, I decided to add some belief work into the equation, which would entail adding affirmations and suggestions. I figured that the relaxed state of meditation would make my mind more open and I knew that it was essential that I start suggesting that my body was good, my being was good, and that there was nothing so wrong about me that I should live in fear of exposure. I could feel the enormous need to absorb these new beliefs into my psyche in order to just make life bearable.

While I could clearly see how some of my present beliefs were making me suffer, I couldn't understand how I had created my illness in the first place, or why I chose such a difficult challenge for myself. It seemed to me, at the time, to have come from out of nowhere. Seth told us that nothing is ever thrust upon us from the outside but is formed on the inside first, through our thoughts and beliefs, until it is finally made physical in reality. But accepting responsibility for my suffering seemed impossible. I felt the rightness of the Seth teachings, yet it was hard for me to accept that everyone who suffered was creating their own situation. How could my power have worked so against me?

I decided that I would have to take a closer look at the years prior to my illness. Who was I as a child, what did I feel, and behind that, what did I believe?

As I began to look back, all the mystery came out of the picture and the truth was perfectly clear.

I had always been frightened as a child. I didn't realize that I was scared, I thought that everyone felt the same way I did. I existed in waves of anxiousness, experiencing that feeling referred to as "butterflies," a jumpy, nervous feeling in the pit of my stomach, on and off throughout the day.

I don't know when these fears began. I was told that the first two years of my life were draining to everyone around me, because I wailed and screamed from a bad case of colic. I joke sometimes, and call the colic the forerunner to ileitis. They certainly produce similar symptoms, and it's interesting to me that I was plagued at birth with the same kind of intestinal pain as with my first disease. If, in fact, nothing happens from the outside alone, then, at a point as early as birth, a being can possess beliefs that interfere with the smooth functioning of his or her body!

As I looked back, I couldn't blame my parents for the fear that engulfed me as a child. It seemed larger and greater than them. Although they both strove to raise me in a loving and secure environment, my feelings prevailed. Of course at the time I was basically unaware of these feelings. I lived around them because they were a part of my being. I felt frightened in many situations, and safest when my mother was in sight.

I can still remember, rather vividly, my first day at nursery school. Mother took me to "Happy Hours" with the hope that they would be happy hours for me. The teacher amused me with a piece of clay, figuring it would make me forget my mother, and encouraged my mother to leave. What she didn't know was that I had radar on my mother, and, when all of a sudden the clay seemed to disappear in my hands, I knew my mother was gone. Panic turned into tears, which flowed uncontrollably until I knew that my mother was on her way back to the school. Only then was I willing to lie down on my Bow Wow blanket and eat a few gumdrops.

By the time I entered kindergarten I knew that I couldn't get away with being such a baby in school and began to suppress the impulse to cry. Although this wasn't always possible, and I sometimes had to bear the embarrassment of crying in class, from an early age I learned how to suppress my emotions.

Throughout my growing up, although I was not aware of what it was, I had a general fear that I projected in many different directions. For example, I would begin feeling uneasy on Sunday afternoons, dreading leaving home on Monday mornings. Because I was so tense by Monday morning I found it impossible to eat breakfast before leaving for school.

I was uptight about the school bus. I feared that I would miss it in the mornings and be unable to find it after school. My greatest fear was that if I couldn't find it after school, I would never get back home again. Of course this was totally irrational as the buses lined up in front of the school every afternoon, waited for a least fifteen minutes after school dismissal, and sported a sign in the window marked with the number of the bus.

But at the time, this fear was bigger than life. I was nervous about academic tests and about the fact that I was seldom completely prepared for my classes. I was constantly distracted by my fears in class, paying little or no attention to my teachers at all as I ran through in my mind how I would get home after school, or face some other crisis.

Life for me was a series of these anxious feelings. I took them for granted because they were such a familiar part of me. I went away to summer camp for seven summers, always going through enormous trauma about leaving home. I learned how to conceal it from everyone, including, at times, myself. Not that I didn't feel it. But I didn't think it was something that I could ever change, it was so natural to me.

Often I have thought about being taught to read and write, add and subtract, punctuate and diagram sentences, dissect frogs--the list goes on and on--but I never attended a class that dealt with who I was or what I felt. Self-examination and exploration were the furthest things from the academic curriculum, which in turn produced many intelligent yet unfulfilled people. It was clear to me that although I had learned how to act right, dress well, get through my studies, and fit in socially, my childhood consisted of one emotional trauma after another. Of course I understand that I was not the only frightened child who ever grew up in this world, and that every child who is frightened does not become ill. However, the anxiety I lived with for sixteen years prior to becoming ill, played a key role in causing my sickness. That anxiety, which centered in my abdomen, was the very same place where my ileitis would eventually grow. The dis-ease grew into disease. This process did not happen overnight. Long before the first symptoms of ileitis became apparent, my fear and anxiety were setting the stage for my intestines to become inflamed.

Once I saw the connection between my dis-ease and disease, I could no longer deny it, and yet it seemed less of a burden than I thought it would. It wasn't as if I had asked to be sick because I wanted to hurt myself. Illness was the only effect my energy could have because it had no other escape or release. Even now, if I experience a nerve-racking event, my intestines can get upset and send me more frequently to the bathroom. If I were to sustain that same kind of nervous energy again, every day of my life, I know that I would be inviting ileitis. Although I could remember my tension, and see its results in my body, I still didn't understand the beliefs that were responsible for so much of my fear.

Then on the evening of July 12, 1975, Jane had a class. By now I knew everyone who was a regular member and noticed that there was a student there who had not been coming regularly. I thought he looked familiar. Although nine months had passed since my first Seth class, I thought he just might be the Kurt Vonnegut guy. We took notice of each other.

Then Seth came through, and I was immediately drawn into his words. "As long as you believe that you dwell in a universe that is a threat, you must defend yourself against it."

Seth spent most of the evening speaking to us about our beliefs in an unsafe universe, and how we believe our world and our species to be unsafe and untrustworthy. "Now, the one-line official consciousness with which you are familiar says, 'The world is not safe. I cannot trust it. Nor can I trust the conditions of experience or the conditions of my own existence, nor can I trust myself.'"

As I listened, Seth's words rang true. I began to see an image of myself as Chicken Little, (a character in a children's story that I read as a child) running through my childhood, shouting internally, "The sky is falling, the sky is falling," without saying it out loud. How crystal clear it all appeared to me now. I had never analyzed it before, but as a child I rarely, if ever, felt completely safe. That is why I worried so. The more I examined my life, the more apparent it became. If I had not felt unsafe, I would not have feared so much danger in all the events of my life, nor would I have experienced so much tension and anxiety in my body. Again, I had no idea of the origin of this fear. My parents, especially my mother, created such a protective loving environment that I could not blame them.

When I was a small child I believed in the magic of the universe. I believed in fairy tales and in the possibility of miracles. The world seemed to be full of color and song. As I grew into adolescence I was confronted with the world of facts, current events, and "real reality," which I was taught was the only clear and correct picture of reality. My dreams and fairy tales had nothing to do with the official world in which I had my existence. Although I had always resisted reading the newspaper or listening to the news on television, as a young woman I basically came to accept the picture of reality that the official world presented. From that time on it was as if something had died inside of me. The world became more black and white and ominous.

It was only after my four years of illness that I began to question the limits of that black and white world again. It was clear to me that I had to go beyond the official world of doctors and medicine in my desperate search for a cure and that I had returned with a lot more than I had bargained for. Along with receiving enough healing energy to start the healing process in my liver, I also opened the door into the world of inner, spiritual exploration. I was peeling the onion of my own psyche and finding that so much of my suffering was, although unconscious, self-induced. I had a lot of work to do, but I finally had some sense of direction.

Chapter Six

How the Utilization of These Ideas Changed my Life

After many months of reading and studying the Seth teachings, I realized that I had to deal with my feelings of fear and inadequacy. I therefore decided to make up my own program to use on a daily basis. After using meditation and breathing as a means of relaxing and quieting my mind, I added both visualization and suggestion work. Each day I implanted the belief that my being was good and that my universe was safe and in this way I begin the process of changing my beliefs. Obviously this doesn't happen overnight, and I still work with my beliefs to this day. As a result, however, I am less afraid of experience and more satisfied with myself.

Because the issues of worth and safety were so crucial for me, my life began to change subtly in response to the new suggestions. I gradually began to come out of my shell. Tentatively I began to talk about my operation.

On May 11, 1976, my father died unexpectedly of a heart attack. My mother, my siblings, and I experienced shock and grief as we came together to share our huge loss. Herman Perl had been so strong and vital that we could not imagine life without him. His death precipitated a lot of changes.

In November of that year Steve and I separated. It was he who finally said we could no longer go on in this unfulfilling relationship. Although I had secretly hoped for something like this, the prospect of losing Steve and my life on the farm, coming, as it did, so soon after losing my father, frightened me. Steve and I discussed the impossibility of continuing our marriage. We both knew that we had been lacking way too much joy and satisfaction. Although we truly cared for each other, our marriage was not nourishing enough for either of us.

Oddly, I felt terrified and grateful at the same time. I knew that Steve was giving me the second chance I had wanted. I realized that if I had made the move, I would have been responsible for destroying the business we ran on our farm. I would have felt terribly guilty about doing that to Steve. Now, with him making that move, I was free to embark on a new life, without guilt. As he drove me back to my mother's home I told him that I knew someday I would thank him, but at that moment I felt disoriented and confused.

When I awoke the next day, I felt even more confused and lost. I was used to my life with Steve and I had no idea what I would do with myself now. I had lived in the country for four years, feeling closer to my animals than to most people. I was still close to my sister and brothers, who had all spent time with Steve and me at the farm. As far as friends went, however, I had few.

I knew, however, that the time had come to begin a new life for myself.

I decided to move to Manhattan. I knew Greenwich Village would be right for me, and so I went about the business of finding an apartment. It was only six months after my father's death and my mother was confused as she rode the subways with me to see some apartments. Six months ago we were both married women, and now here we were looking at tiny dives that my mother thought weren't fit for a rat. I felt excited, exhilarated, and scared.

I sublet a small, furnished apartment on Carmine Street and on December 1 moved in with my four small dogs--much to my mother's apprehension. I was ready to begin a new life, on my own. With the removal of my father's strong hand from my life, I felt truly on my own.

During this time I called Jane to inform her about the separation. She was very warm and supportive, supplying me with names and phone numbers of some of the regular class members who lived in New York City. She told me that she felt that one in particular would be very helpful to me.

I called Rich Kendall that night and within a very short time we became close friends. Rich was easy to talk to, enormously playful and funny. He seemed to know everyone who had attended the Seth classes and he introduced me to a lot of other people as well. I also dated occasionally. I began to think about meaningful ways to spend my time. I continued with my daily meditation and belief work, and all the while my life was changing around me.

I still found it frightening to tell people, especially men, about my ileostomy, but I was telling them nonetheless. I discovered that few people were as critical as I. Moreover, my beliefs about my body had changed more than I had realized. I still saw my ileostomy as a problem, but I made a separation in my mind between it and me. I knew now that my being amounted to more than any one part, and that although I was not particularly happy about this part, it didn't on the other hand diminish my value or beauty. I began to believe that I deserved to be loved by someone whose love I could easily return, and I did not feel that I would marry again unless I fell deeply in love.

I started to consider the idea of teaching Seth classes. I assumed that a lot of people were interested in Seth who had never had the opportunity to attend regular Seth classes during the time in which Jane held them.

I phoned Jane to ask her what she thought about the idea of my teaching. I was delighted to hear that she was all for it. I began to organize my ideas.

In January of 1977 I was using the Ouija board by myself, trying to get information for a troubled friend. The board kept spelling out the kind of motherly advice I would have given my friend. I felt rather foolish, as if I were making the entire communication up in my head. Then the planchette moved to the letter G and at the same time the name Jerry popped into my mind. "Does the name Jerry mean anything to you?" I asked my friend Larry, who replied that it had no meaning for him at all. But I couldn't help thinking about that name. "Doesn't the name Jerry begin with a J?" I thought. "Why would the planchette pick out the letter G if the name I'm getting in my head is Jerry?" Throughout the next day this bothered me; somehow I couldn't get it out of my mind.

Later that day Rich came by to see me. He told me of a friend of his, who, like the rest of us, was very much into the Seth material. He said that his friend had expressed a strong interest in meeting me. He went on to describe him in great detail, and then asked if he should give him my phone number. "Well, what's his name?" I asked, to which Rich replied, "Jerry."

"Give him the number," I said without hesitation.

Jerry contacted me a day later. We made a date to meet the following evening at my apartment and then go out to eat in the neighborhood. It turned out that Jerry lived just two blocks away.

I liked him immediately. He was tall, dark, and handsome, and exuded a sense of strength and trust. He was intelligent, and more important to me, he knew a lot about Seth and creating your own reality. When I told him I planned to teach a Seth class, he was supportive and enthusiastic. He offered to make me copies of all his Seth tapes, which was a wonderful idea. I had only recorded a few sessions myself and hadn't yet figured out a format for my classes. It now occurred to me that the Seth tapes could be the finest teaching tool imaginable. We talked and figured out that he had stopped attending Seth classes regularly around the time that I began attending, which explained why I had met so many of his friends and not him. He was in the first year of law school, and was also in business with his father.

I hadn't consciously planned to become seriously involved with anyone so quickly after ending a seven-year marriage. But Jerry was so special. He had unique qualities that drew me to him. I found that the other men I met didn't affect me like

Jerry did and I sensed that this relationship could possibly be an important one for me.

I decided to tell Jerry about the ileostomy right away. In the past I had always waited until the very last minute, but Jerry was different. On our first date we spent the evening talking and getting to know each other and I felt that we were, above all, open and honest with each other. We spoke about my illness. I didn't have the courage to talk about the surgery. I did tell Jerry that there was something I wanted to tell him, but did not feel comfortable to talk about yet. I remember feeling concerned that this knowledge might scare him away. By our second date, a few evenings later, I knew we were both looking at a potentially serious relationship, and if Jerry couldn't handle the ileostomy, I wanted to know now. I had grown enough to believe that any man who couldn't handle my situation wasn't man enough for me. Nonetheless I feared rejection.

By the time he arrived at my apartment I was pacing the floor. Lighting up one cigarette after another, I let Jerry into my small apartment and told him I had to talk about my problem. He sat down on the couch and listened intently as I fumbled around, trying to find pleasant words to describe what to me was a most unpleasant situation.

Jerry tried hard to keep his composure. I saw his eyes glance away from me momentarily as he began to get the picture, but for the most part he was difficult to read. We went out to dinner and basically had a nice evening, but we were both subdued. Jerry had been caught off guard and was now trying to sort through all that I had told him. I was afraid that I would lose him after all, and I felt naked and embarrassed. "Maybe I should have waited to tell him until he liked me more," I thought, but I knew this wasn't true. Relationships had to be handled openly and honestly from the start.

I didn't see or hear from Jerry for two weeks. I called and invited him once to dinner but he declined. He said he was going skiing for a couple of days and would call me when he returned. During this time I concluded that Jerry and I would probably just be friends. Although I hadn't completely given up on him, I felt he was backing away. I decided he was a nice guy to have as a friend, though, and I should definitely take him up on his offer to make Seth tapes for my class. With that in mind I called him the next Monday morning. To my surprise he said he was just about to call me and ask me out to dinner.

We had a nice time, but I still couldn't read him. He seemed to be interested in me, but he was holding back. I didn't know if this was because he cared about me and feared coming on too strong, or if he wasn't all that interested. Maybe he just wanted to pursue a friendship with me. But I knew I wanted more than friendship with him.

February 5, 1977, was my twenty-sixth birthday. I gave myself a party and invited all my new friends. Of course that included Jerry.

Needless to say, I was very jumpy. I knew Jerry and I would spend a night together soon, or not at all. Something had to give in this relationship. The vibrations between us were not what I would call platonic.

The party was scheduled for eight P.M. By nine practically everyone had arrived, except Jerry. My fear that he might not come at all mounted as ten o'clock approached. Finally at about ten-thirty he arrived with two friends who he said had kept him waiting. "Likely story," I thought, but I was enormously relieved anyway. The remainder of the party was filled with anticipation for both Jerry and me. When the last guest said good night we were finally alone. We both knew that the time had come for us to become lovers. Naturally we both felt ill at ease and I was reluctant to remove my clothing. My neighbor had lent me a sexy negligee that covered my appliance adequately, and this was how I dressed for bed that night, and for many years to come.

That night sealed the bond between us. We have been together ever since. I now had a satisfying relationship. My next intention was to begin filling my need for meaningful work.

I remember how fearful my mother was on the night that I opened my door to ten strangers who had answered my ad in the Village Voice about a Seth class. I had only spoken to these people on the phone, but felt certain that I would have no problems. The class went beautifully. I am still in contact with some of these people.

The classes became ongoing. Because of the enormous interest in Seth, I began to receive numerous phone calls from people who heard about the classes. I believe they were helpful and inspirational to many people, and certainly they helped me continue to build upon my positive beliefs. Listening week after week to Seth speak about the value of my being, my worth and right to joy, further reinforced my sense of power. I began to feel more confident. I made sure I meditated and worked with my beliefs daily.

As time went on, my self-awareness grew. I could now look into my mind every morning and see the beliefs that were seeding my emotions. Every time emotions seemed to come upon me that I didn't understand, I could discover their source within my beliefs. I also came to see the same two key issues underlying most of the others that arose: either I felt I wasn't good enough, that my energy was not to be trusted, or that I wasn't safe enough, and the universe was not to be trusted. As I continued to work with the ideas that my being was good as well as safe, I found that I was becoming a more happy and secure person.

In the spring of 1977, I moved into Jerry's apartment and that fall we moved to a larger, more comfortable space. There I taught Seth classes twice a month and held many private sessions. I felt now, for the first time in my life, that I was where I wanted to be, doing what I wanted to do. Jerry and I were beginning to understand each other, and I felt content and complete in our life together. I had love, meaningful work, a wonderful family, and a terrific group of friends. Jerry and I were married on September 15, 1979, in Las Vegas, shortly after my divorce became final. The only incomplete part of the picture was the ileostomy. Although I could accept it more, it was still a source of sadness for me. Yet I honestly couldn't imagine undergoing surgery again. All I remembered of surgery was enormous pain and sickness. I was certain that I would always be denied surgery to reconnect my bowel.

On the night of September 29, 1979, Jane Roberts held a small Seth class in her home. It was the last class that I attended, the last tape and transcript that I acquired. As always we were all enthralled by the power of Seth's wisdom and love as he spoke to us about trusting our everyday impulses. He spoke to Jerry, whom he had always referred to as "the Indian," instructing him to trust his impulses in our marriage.

As the evening drew to a close we mingled and talked. At this time Sue Watkins walked over to Jerry and told him that he still reminded her of Kurt Vonnegut. My ears perked up in excitement as I realized what was taking place. I hadn't even thought about the Kurt Vonnegut business since the day Jerry and I had met. And here I was married to him! How amazing, I thought, that I had felt so much for him on our first meeting in Jane's kitchen. How incredible the way our inner self knows and feels things before our conscious mind knows anything. My number-one dream had come true. I wondered whether any of this could have happened if I hadn't changed my beliefs. In my heart I knew that it couldn't have, and that all of this was the reward.

In January of 1982 Jerry and I adopted our first son. Because I had never used birth control and had never missed a period, I assumed I was not overly fertile. I felt that my body, which was maintained by a lot less intestine than the average person's, had its own wisdom and would have conceived if it wanted to. I therefore had no desire to pursue any medical treatment to bring about conception, and began to ask the universe to deliver my children to me through another means.

I meet many people who make painful choices to avoid adopting a child because they believe a relationship with an adopted child is somehow less sacred than a biological one. I feel sorry for them. The bond that I share with my children is stronger than blood. It is another example of how our beliefs determine the conditions of our lives, what happens to us, and what does not.

Fortunately, Jerry and I now have a beautiful family, which has given us enormous joy and satisfaction. Being a mother has added a deeply nourishing dimension to my life. We lost our second son to an overdose in 2008, which I have written about in my book "Lost and Found---A Mother Connects-Up With Her Son In Spirit." Nonetheless, each day I live I am grateful for the lives of my children, both on earth and in spirit.

Chapter Eight

Reconnective Surgery

When my first son was fourteen months old, from seemingly out of the blue, I developed a case of hives. I started breaking out with enormous swellings that forced my eyes shut and my body to itch all over.

Looking back at it now I believe that there was probably no connection whatsoever, but at the time the only explanation I could think of was that my rectum, which had not been removed in the last surgery, was causing the disruption. Although I never wanted to hear about it, my doctors had warned me that a rectum, left in the body yet disconnected from the rest of the bowels, was a dangerous thing. Dr. Marvin had always been in favor of removal, but I couldn't bring myself to do it. The doctors told me that a disconnected rectum could become cancerous and for the most part, I ignored them, but now I was frightened. I had always argued that no part of my body was going to become ill, connected or not, as my blood still flowed into it and my blood was too full of healthy beliefs to fail me now. But I wondered. Could these hives be showing me that something really terrible was happening in my body? Could I, in fact, be unhealthy?

As the result of the hives and my fear, I allowed myself to be examined for bowel disease for the first time in many years. All of my "favorite" tests were run. The results showed that my bowels were one hundred percent healthy and not related to the hives. My fears rose again, however, when a few days later Dr. Marvin informed me that he wasn't pleased with the result of one of my blood tests. He said that it seemed to indicate liver illness, and that further blood tests as well as a sonogram were necessary.

My first reaction was anger. I vehemently told him that I would not be further tested and that I knew that I was well. However, soon my anger gave way to fear as the doctor said that I shouldn't try to hide from the truth. "Think it over," he said, "and call me back." I hung up and found myself overwhelmed with different reactions.

I was experiencing plenty of energy and exuberance. How could I feel so much energy if my liver was in serious trouble? Isn't liver disease always accompanied by weakness? And furthermore, when I submitted to blood tests ten years back, hadn't Dr. Marvin then found the same liver abnormality? At the time my family and I had undergone a week-long scare, waiting for results from a second, more extensive set of blood tests.

I was living on my farm in Chemung then, experiencing the same doubts and fears as now. I paced back and forth in the kitchen, waiting for that inevitable phone call that would tell me if I was well.

Two nights before I received the test results in Chemung, I had a dream. Jane Roberts appeared to me and said, "If you believed in the validity of your own experience, then you would know that you are well. You would trust what you know and you would have no fear of the blood test!" The results showed that I still tested positive for the Hepatitis C virus, however, my liver functions were normal. It was only then that I realized that the spiritual healing had not destroyed the virus, although it had rendered it powerless.

This was obviously the same abnormality that Dr. Marvin had seen in the past. I finally understood that the abnormality showed up because I still had the virus and that for the remainder of my life these enzymes would remain a little bit elevated. However, everything else regarding my liver looked good, and so I decided not to worry about it. The hives cleared up a week later. It was now Spring of 1983 and I decided when the Fall rolled around I would take on the challenge and explore reconnecting my bowel.

Right after Thanksgiving my mother and I went to see Doctors Baum and Marvin. It was wonderful to see David after all these years. Although more than a decade had passed, he didn't look a day older. I was confident that he would give me his best advice. I had already chosen not to use him as my surgeon, not because I didn't trust him, but because I wanted to eliminate all past associations surrounding surgery.

I told David of my desire to deal with this situation once and for all. I asked him if he thought reconnection was possible, and if it was advisable. He said that it might work, but I would have to bear in mind that if it didn't, the ileostomy would have to be made permanent by removal of my rectum. The idea of going through surgery twice, only to end up where I had been, seemed like an unbearable punishment to me...and yet how could I not take the chance?

My mother then asked David if he knew exactly how much colon I had left. We both remembered Barry saying, just after the surgery, that not enough tissue remained to make the temporary opening and that David had done something unusual. David said that there was enough tissue to warrant reconnection. Dr. Marvin disagreed. He felt that the amount of diarrhea I would have to live with after the reconnection was done could make me a slave to the bathroom. He also mentioned the greater risk of recurrence with reconnection. That did not concern me. What did concern me was the idea of living in the bathroom.

However, we had been merely seeking advice and we weren't planning to use either David or Dr. Marvin. I wanted to hear from the people who might actually do the work. Dan Present and Irwin Gelernt had both been strongly recommended to us. The first was known to be one of the best gastroenterologists in Manhattan, and the second was reputed to be a brilliant surgeon.

I phoned Dr. Present's office the next day, but he wasn't available. That night at nine our phone rang, and an easy pleasant voice introduced himself as Dan Present. I poured out my entire story (including my experience with Harry Edwards and healing). Dan listened, said he couldn't comment on my healing story but that reconnection was certainly possible. When confronted with my fears concerning diarrhea, he explained that there were medications to regulate such conditions. He allayed my fears about the amount of colon I had remaining. His confidence was infectious. He approved highly of Dr. Gelernt and said he'd be happy to work with him, and often did.

When Dr. Present saw my X rays, he said that I certainly had enough ileum left for reconnection. After a general examination, he said I appeared to be in very good health. The next step would be for me to see Dr. Gelernt, while Dr. Present would review the results of my blood tests. When we left the doctor's office I began to wrestle with my fears. I did not know it, but I was about to face the last struggle with my resistance to surgery.

"This is craziness," I thought, "my life is going fine. If I take a chance with this surgery, I could make a mess of things. I've already gone through the toughest years with an ileostomy, made all the adjustments when they were most difficult to make. Why should I bother to try and change it now?" There were a zillion reasons for me to forget the whole idea, but I knew that I could not. One way or another the internal structure of my bowels had to be altered. Either I could attempt to reconnect my rectum to my ileum, or opt to remove my rectum completely.

Feeling very upset and frightened that evening, I informed Jerry and my mother that I was going to forget about the entire situation. I was certain that I could not deal with the surgery. I would put the matter off for a few years and worry about it then. In my own mind I knew that I was growling and blowing off steam, but it felt comforting to assume that I had the choice to call the whole thing off anytime I wanted to.

When I awoke in the morning I felt quite different. If I was going to deal with this situation, and I was, then I certainly wanted to try to reconnect my rectum. Somehow in the light of day all of this seemed attainable.

For the first time in years I indulged in fantasies of what it would feel like to possess my old body again. Before I knew what was happening, I had my heart set on reconnection. My new concern was that the doctors would discover some reason to discourage me.

I liked Dr. Gelernt. He exuded knowledge and confidence. I passed his inspection, and he saw no reason preventing me from undergoing reconnective surgery. He looked in his calendar, said that he could make time and scheduled me for two weeks after the new year. Then we returned to Dr. Present's office. Dan confirmed that my blood tests checked out normally and agreed that we should go ahead with the surgery. He even said that if he had seen me in the past, he would have encouraged me to take this action sooner.

Nothing stood in my way now. We were in the middle of December, and I had only one month to wait. During this time I went through a lot of ups and downs, but, having made up my mind to face surgery, I didn't falter again. All of a sudden my ileostomy annoyed me more.

During this time Doctors Gelernt and Present tried to obtain my past medical records. Oddly, none seemed to exist. Dr. Gelernt assumed that because I had a temporary ileostomy, I must have at least one foot of colon attached to my rectum.

I checked into Mt. Sinai Hospital in Manhattan on January 10, 1984. I remember it as if it was yesterday. With my arm wrapped tightly around Jerry's we walked slowly down the long hospital corridor as an orderly took us up to my room, complete with a view of the park. "I may be reduced to helplessness for a while," I thought, "but I'm going to walk out of here on my own two feet." As a result of working with my beliefs, I had found the courage to face what at one time seemed impossible to me. I was scared, but not too scared to make this change in my life.

As I walked slowly up to my room, savoring those last few

moments before I became a patient, I could barely believe what I was doing. I didn't know where the courage came to go through with this, but it was there.

In retrospect, I can see that my ability to face this reality was fostered by my working with my beliefs, particularly in the area of safety. Years of addressing the issue of fear had lightened fear's hold upon me. By suggesting to myself that I was safe and protected, I slowly whittled away at my fear until I was free to take this action.

As I sat in my hospital bed, waiting for the stretcher that would take me down the long corridor to the surgical rooms, I was amazed at my composure and confidence. My family surrounded me, as my siblings and I chanted together. I felt reassured that my healer friend in Britain, Ray Branch, had been informed of the surgery. Ray had worked with Harry Edwards for many years prior to Harry's death in 1976. I knew that Ray would direct all the help possible to me now. My family, friends, and students sent their love, and when the stretcher finally did come to collect me, my attitude was one of faith and trust. "Put me out and do your thing to me," I thought, "I will trust that I will be safe."

My mother and Jerry walked alongside my stretcher for as long as they were allowed, and then we kissed good-bye, just in front of the restricted area.

As usual I waited on my stretcher for something to happen, wishing that the sedative had made me less aware. I few minutes later I was wheeled into an operating room. I remember Dr. Gelernt walking in and the huge surge of confidence I felt. "Please put me together again," I thought.

I had made Jerry promise that he would come into the recovery room as soon as he was allowed. I wanted to know if the surgery had been successful. I had an eerie feeling that the situation inside my body might not be just as it should. I didn't fear illness, but I did worry about the amount of tissue remaining. I remembered what Barry had said back in 1969 about the temporary hook-up. I couldn't help wondering if Dr. Gelernt was going to find what he expected. I kept saying that I feared he would discover a can of worms inside and hoped that things were going to work out. When Dr. Gelernt opened me up, he did not find the foot of colon he expected to find. Instead he found four inches of colon connected to twenty-one inches of ileum, an unusual hook-up indeed. Apparently in my last surgery David found himself with too little colon to make a temporary hook-up. He didn't have the heart to remove my rectum, either, which would have rendered the ileostomy irreversible. He therefore connected ileum to colon in order to make the piece of remaining disconnected tissue longer. In this way he was able to create a temporary hook-up by substituting ileum for colon. Nonetheless, when Dr. Gelernt discovered this, he could have decided against reconnection. The colon is the large bowel and the ileum is the small bowel. They work differently. The colon works as a reservoir. It holds water. How much water could a four-inch colon hold? Dr. Gelernt took all of this into consideration and chose to reconnect my bowel.

When I became aware in the recovery room, I somehow knew that my bowel had been reconnected. How I knew this, I still don't understand. Soon Jerry was allowed to see me and he confirmed my feeling and told me everything looked fine. I was greatly relieved that the pain from the surgery was certainly bearable. It had nothing in common with my former surgeries.

The next two weeks were not easy ones--except compared to what I had feared them to be. My brother Richard, who lived near the hospital, visited early every morning to check my progress or massage my feet. I came to rely on his encouragement and visits throughout the long days of recovery. Naturally I felt quite ill. My bowels did not work for about ten days, and when they did I could barely find my way out of the bathroom. Fortunately, within a few days, my doctors started giving me medication to slow down bowel function. It made all the difference in the world. What could have been an unbearable living situation changed radically. For the first time in many years I came to see that medicine could be a marvelous thing.

You can imagine the feelings of deep satisfaction and liberation I felt as a result of this final surgery after fifteen years of living with an ileostomy.

I know now that I will need to take medication for the rest of my life. Normal colons are ten feet long; mine is only four inches. Considering this, I feel grateful for the medication that makes my colon behave as if it were normal. Perhaps someday my colon will function better and I will need less of the medication, but I am not concerned about it. The medication is a very small price to pay for liberation from my ileostomy.

On the other hand, I want to make it clear that I do not see living with an ileostomy as the worst thing in the world. To be perfectly honest, since the event of reconnective surgery, my life has changed very little. I'm married to the same man, and I am dedicated to the same work and family. I've maintained most of the same friends and interests. Of course I experience a physical and psychological freedom that I do appreciate. If I had been stronger, however, I might have been able to achieve it anyway. The fact is, the most important aspects of my life have not changed.

When I look back on my ileostomy, I can see how in many ways, it was positive. Certainly it, and my entire bout with illness, made me question what really matters in life, and what does not. I came to see that how you view what happens to you is much more important than what actually happens. If you truly love and trust yourself, you can learn how to make the most out of life, even if life doesn't always go as you had intended it.

Adversity can go a long way toward developing values and priorities. Life-threatening situations make you focus on what matters most to you. The petty annoyances of life are no longer worth bothering about. The key here is to realize and focus upon what brings joy and satisfaction to you and those around you. Adversity need not be a prerequisite to straightening out your beliefs and attitudes. Examining and changing limiting beliefs, however, is a prerequisite to good health and a satisfying life experience. As you can see from observing my life, as I began to change my beliefs, the scope of my experience altered radically. I became less afraid to be myself and was able to try new experiences. I am not saying that things never go wrong in my life, or that I never experience unhappiness. I lost a son when he was 22 to an overdose. I know the pain of attending my own child's funeral. I am saying, however, that my overall experience is joyful.

The same will hold true for you. As you work with altering negative personal beliefs, you become a better friend to yourself, kinder and more supportive. When things go wrong in your life, you don't resort to self-blame and criticism. You will find that you are able to make changes that at one time you thought were impossible. I hope that through observing my life, you will feel encouraged about the possibilities for change that exist within your own!

Chapter Nine

The Sheri Perl Spiritual Healing Program

Over the years I put together my own healing program combining the techniques and ideas I had accumulated from years of study and working with teachers in the field. From Harry Edwards to Ram Dass, those techniques that worked best for me and that I still use today, were woven into a cohesive meditation/healing program that I think you will find very useful.

The program always begins with The Gatekeeper Meditation technique. This teaches you to focus your awareness on your breath, which allows you to take a step back from your usual stance, which is right in the center of your daily thoughts and concerns. Once you are able to do that, there are numerous avenues to explore. I will teach you the different techniques and once you are comfortable with them, you can pick and choose what it is you would like to work on.

Back in 1971, when I first experienced the power of distant healing energy, I was floored by what it could do, and certain that Harry Edwards was some kind of God. Although I wanted desperately to become involved in the work, I didn't believe that a mere human being, with all the imperfections that I knew I had, could ever utilize such powerful forces. When I was told in a reading with medium Glenn Dove in 1999 that Harry was around me (Harry passed in 1976) and that I could do what he had done, I was completely overjoyed and completely skeptical! Although at times it is easy to question abilities that cannot be seen, I persevere, practicing what I know and making it available to others.

It is my sincere hope that this healing program will get you started on a path of self-healing that will indeed expand to help others. The healing program will get you started using both "Hands-on Healing" as well as "Distant Healing." I work with all of the following modalities now, and I am convinced that you can too.

The program works with two very valuable components: the energy that exists both around and inside us, and the nuts and bolts of our own thinking minds. Lets get to it!

Step One
Meditation Technique - The Gatekeeper

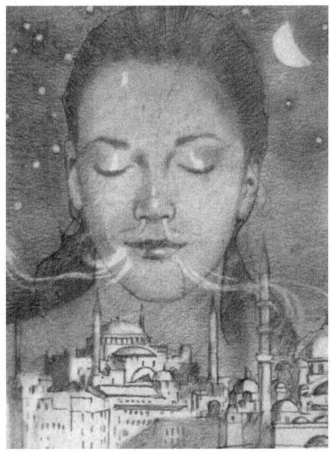

Illustration by Robert C. Sabin

After years of trying out different meditation techniques I learned the following technique from listening to a Ram Dass lecture series on CD called "Spiritual Awakening." As soon as I heard it, it appealed to me because I liked its use of breath, but more than that, I liked the introduction of the gatekeeper. It really helped me to zero in on my breath and it goes like this:

1. Start by finding a comfortable place where you can remove yourself from the everyday distractions of your life. You can sit or lie down, depending on what is more comfortable for you.

2. Focus all of your attention at the tip of your nose.

3. Imagine that you are the gatekeeper at the entrance to a big city and that it is your very important job to watch the coming and going of your breath.

4. Breathe in through your nose and feel the cool air as it enters at the tip of your nostrils.

5. Exhale through your nose and feel the warm air as it leaves your nostrils.

6. Breathing in cool, breathing out warm. Breathing in cool, breathing out warm. In cool. Out warm. In cool. Out warm.

7. At some point you will realize that you have lost the feeling of your breath coming and going. That will be because your mind has wandered. When you realize this, simply return your focus to the tip of your nose and resume your position as gatekeeper.

8. Repeat this for at least 5 to 10 minutes, returning time and time again to the breath.

Learning The Gatekeeper Meditation, (or any meditation

technique that works for you) is a crucial tool for expanding your awareness. Until you learn to "cultivate the witness" which means to view your thoughts from a witness perspective, you will not necessarily be conscious of what you are thinking. Without you even knowing it, at times you will be a slave to thoughts that run you wily-nilly all over the place. From where you've got to be, to what you've got to do, it is easy to get lost in what author and meditation teacher Stephen Levine calls "The Under-dream," that constant stream of thoughts that keeps, at least, a portion of your mind engaged at all times. The fact is, the thinking mind likes to think and we are addicted to listening to it. Unfortunately, we become lost in the under-dream and don't realize that we are diluting our perceptions of the present moment because we are so distracted. Try this:

Meditation in Action

Usually TGM (The Gatekeeper Meditation) is practiced while you are sitting quietly and doing nothing. I have found, however, that using TGM while involved in my day is awesome because it takes me out of the under-dream, and allows me to be more present in the moment. Once I am no longer lost in the under-dream, everything becomes richer and fuller. It's like cutting out the middle-man in my mind who is always busy commenting on everything and drawing my attention away from the present moment and into itself.

One day, while I was getting my hair shampooed at the beauty shop, I spontaneously started to focus on my breathing. All of sudden, the warm water and gentle hands on my head felt like heaven. I had never experienced a shampoo like it before! It felt mesmerizing and I thought to myself, "Wow, if only I could be present like this all the time." So I decided to see what it would feel like if I used TGM while doing other things like eating or taking a bath and I just couldn't believe it! It was as if I was waking up inside my reality and finding a much richer experience. Yes, your mind will wander and yes, you will have to remind yourself to return to breath, but each time you do, your perceptions are heightened.

Step Two
Working with Healing Energy - Focused Breathing

Focused Breathing is something that I learned from Harry Edwards, although his name for it was "Characterized Breathing." Harry explained that by combining deep breathing with visualization you could literally begin to work with the energies that, in Harry's words, "eddy about us."

We have already talked about the fact that there are radio waves and television waves in the atmosphere, all around us, that we cannot see. In the same vein, there are many energy forces that exist in the atmosphere all around us that, similarly, we cannot see. By adding visualization to our deep breathing we can begin to work with that energy, first by drawing it into ourselves for self-healing and then directing it outward to others.

This is what I do when I want to activate some healing energy. Sometimes I'm tired and need a little jump start. I use this technique to boost my energy, relieve discomfort and direct energy to others. It works like this:

1. Start by finding a comfortable place where you can remove yourself from the everyday distractions of your life. You can sit or lie down, depending on what is more comfortable for you.

2. Begin by using The Gatekeeper Meditation.

3. Once you are feeling the cool and warm air as it enters and leaves your nostrils begin to add your visualization.

- As you inhale cool air, envision drawing streams of healing energy into you.

  Inhaling cool I envision streams of white and golden light entering into me.

4. As you exhale, visualize the energy going through your body. Although the inhale is used strictly to draw healing energy into you, the exhale can be used in many different ways:

- Envision your body being cleansed.

  "Exhaling warm, my body is being cleansed."

- Envision your body releasing all tension.
  "Exhaling warm my body is releasing all tension."

- Envision the energy entering your hands.

  "Exhaling warm I envision this energy entering my hands."

- Envision the energy going outward from you to another.

  "Exhaling warm I see this energy going outward from me and entering into _____."

Remember that this works because you are adding visualization, so allow yourself to visualize. If you are directing energy to another, see that person in your mind and visualize the energy surrounding and entering into them.

Expanding On Focused Breathing

Focused Breathing teaches you how to work with energy to develop your own innate healing abilities. It is the best practice I know for absorbing and directing energy. Energy can be activated when we combine breath with visualization and this practice can energize us as well as help us.

While using FB (Focused Breathing) there are a number of different functions that you can perform and it is your choice what you would like to work on first. You may feel exhausted and simply want some energy, in which case you would envision the energy entering into you on the inhale, and on the exhale, you would envision the energy filling your entire body. If it is stress that you want to work with, you can use the exhale to envision releasing all the stress you are feeling from your body.

Some people find it helpful to work with crystals, which can add to the energy present. Feel free to use whatever helps or appeals to you. I, of course, seek connection with Harry Edwards and others-in-spirit who I believe are present. Each of you have your own guides-in-spirit who will work with you. You only need to ask them for their help to start the process. Staying consistent with this is necessary if you want to develop a committed healing practice.

Years ago, when I was first informed that I could do healing work, I asked Ray Branch, (Harry's close friend and right hand man who carried on the healing work at the sanctuary after Harry's death) what I should actually say when asking for healing for someone. He said to simply ask "Is there anything you can do?" No hocus pocus, no magical prayer or chant, just a straightforward question! I think this is very significant. Over the years I have taken numerous workshops in different healing modalities and was surprised to see how complicated and detailed some of the modalities were. After completing a workshop that was top-heavy with instructions from a to z, I questioned if I could even memorize all the steps and if they were really necessary. I had a reading with medium Glenn Dove and so I asked Harry (through Glenn, of course) what he thought of the workshop and the answer I was given was "flair and pageantry. " Harry always believed in keeping it simple. So, I recommend the same to you. Beware of those programs that turn spiritual healing into a complicated process!

Step Three
Working With Beliefs - Discovering and Reprogramming

There are two parts to Step Three. I think of them as Discovering and Reprogramming. Discovering refers to the time put into observing, noting and jotting down thoughts that habitually arise when you are attempting to focus your attention on your breath. Reprogramming uses what I call "antidote suggestions" that you will construct yourself in order to implement the suggestions needed to counteract your habitual, limiting or negative thoughts.

In a sense we will become our own hypnotists and our own subjects and this is a good thing because each of us could use some positive reprogramming in one area or another. This is because in our childhoods, when we were pretty much open books, we readily accepted and downloaded into our subconscious minds all kinds of suggestions. According to stem cell biologist Bruce Lipton, by the time we are 6 years old we have formulated beliefs that will affect us for the rest of our lives.

We have all been programmed in ways that we can't begin to know and yet we carry the weight of those programs on our shoulders. If we were fortunate to be raised by loving, supportive adults, we may carry less baggage, but whether it was in your home, your school or in your place of worship, none of us have gone unscathed. According to The World Health Organization, globally an estimated 350 million people of all ages suffer from depression. What does that tell you?

For Step Three I suggest that you keep a journal.

Discovering

1. Start by finding a comfortable place where you can remove yourself from the everyday distractions of your life. You can

sit or lie down, depending on what is more comfortable for you.

2. Begin by using The Gatekeeper Meditation

3. Feel the cool air as you inhale and the warm air as you exhale. Keep repeating until you realize that you have lost your awareness of your breath. (Of course this is because your mind has wandered).

4. Gently remind yourself to return your attention to your breath, but take a second to observe what you were thinking about and jot it down.

5. Return to The Gatekeeper and keep repeating this process of breathing, jotting down your thoughts and breathing.

No surprise ... he's always been stupid!	She's too conceited for my blood!	They're all just real selfish snobs!	JUDGING
That mole looks suspicious.	What if I never find a job!	I'll never find a soul mate at my age!	WORRYING
I'll wear black so I'll look more serious.	Better make a list so I don't overspend.	I'll have to stay home until taxes are done.	PLANNING
If only I had a supportive father.	I wish I could come in first ... just once!	If they would listen, they would understand.	WISHING
I'll never look as slim as that woman.	Why can't I get A's like him?	She will always be prettier than me.	COMPARING
These idiots should learn how to drive.	How can they eat out when they're so fat?	She looks so much older than she is.	CRITICIZING

Reprogramming

1. Take out your journal and look at your notes. Observe what you have written down and determine what categories your thoughts fall into. Here is a list of common categories:

- Judging
- Worrying
- Planning
- Wishing
- Comparing
- Criticizing

2. On another page organize your notes so that thoughts that fall under the same category are grouped together. *Sample below.*

3. Observe the kind of thoughts that your mind habitually navigates to. Question those thoughts and determine if they serve you or hurt you.

4. Create an antidote suggestion that we will use to begin the process of reprogramming your beliefs. *See sample below.*

INITIAL THOUGHT	ANTIDOTE
You will never succeed.	I CAN and WILL succeed
You never do anything right.	I do MANY THINGS well.
You are inferior.	I am as GOOD as others.
My body is weak.	My body is STRONG.
I am worthless.	I am a WORTHY, DESERVING person.

5. Choosing two antidotes suggestions to work with first and then return to The Gatekeeper Meditation.

6. Once you have quieted your mind, while inhaling cool, mentally say the first antidote suggestion to yourself.

7. While exhaling warm, mentally say the second antidote suggestion to yourself. Repeat as long as you like up to 10 minutes. Then let it go.

Keep in mind that changing your habitual ways of thinking may take some time. Some beliefs you may be able to let go of instantly, just by seeing that they are beliefs and not facts of reality, but others may linger on. After all, if they are habitual, then you have been carrying them for a long time. You may even find resistance to changing some ideas, simply because the familiar feels safe. But look at everything in front of you and ask yourself, "Do I want to believe this anymore?"

In a sense you are whittling away at old negative beliefs. You might not see any difference immediately, but then again, you may. It will depend on how deeply an idea is ingrained. For me what often happened is that, at some point I would realize that a situation that used to frighten me, wasn't such a big deal anymore.

There is no way to measure this kind of growth. Sometimes you are the only one who will know that anything significant has taken place, but it doesn't matter. You will feel grateful for whatever degree of growth you attain because you will feel the benefit.

More on Working With Beliefs
(The presence of Monkey Mind)

If you are concerned about your habitual thoughts being revealed to you, worry not, for I can assure you that they will be. From the moment you try to sit back and silence your mind you will find that your mind becomes extremely active. This is why so many people believe that they can't meditate. They are under the mis-impression that meditation means attaining a silent mind and, as much as I wish it were that easy, the minute I try to get quiet, my mind immediately comes up with a zillion things for me to think about. As a monkey swings from branch to branch, the monkey mind swings from one thought right into another in its attempt to keep control of you. Most of us are so used to this constant dialogue that we don't even realize we have become lost in thought.

For the Discovery aspect of working with beliefs, we will make use of this monkey mind phenomenon and observe the thoughts as they come up. This, in itself, can make a big difference, for it allows you to see that you are not your thoughts, that you are the awareness in which all those thoughts take place. That realization is huge, for more often than not, we identify with our thoughts and think that they define who we are. They don't. You are not your thoughts, you are the one who is having them, but they are not you!

Once you are able to distinguish between yourself and your thoughts, you can write them down in your journal and observe them objectively.   When I first started this process, I was surprised to see how many thoughts I entertained that I had never examined. Some were things I had been told as a child and had accepted as truth, never thinking twice about their validity or effect on me.

In time I came to see that many of my habitual thoughts were pointing me in the same direction. I decided that in order to uncover what my beliefs were that I needed to evaluate where some of my habitual thoughts stemmed from and so I would ask myself the following question: If these thoughts running through my mind are a plot in a play, what would the name of the play be?   For example, if my mind kept going back to an argument between myself and my boss, the underlying belief would resemble something like, "I can never get along with my boss," in which case the antidote suggestion would be the opposite or "I can get along with my boss very well."

Now, when you first start challenging a belief, you will feel rather doubtful and your mind will come back with "But I can't stand the man and we just don't get along," so you don't stay on this for hours and hours. You do it for 5 to 10 minutes and then you let it go. In time, however, you find that you have nullified the belief, and the charge you feel regarding your boss will begin to weaken.

Now, in some situations you might just be better off looking for another job, but when it comes to personal things, like your weight or your health, you are not going to attain another body and so you need to work with the one you have. If you are overweight and it upsets you, you would start with TGM and once you were less in your thinking mind, more relaxed and open to suggestion, you would start to implement your antidote suggestion which in this case could be: My weight is under control and I feel good about my body. Of course, at first this will sound crazy to you, because you will be directly challenging the reality that you know, but do it anyway. Do it for a few minutes and then let it go.

Now, common sense tells you that as all-powerful as beliefs can be, they don't work alone. In this case watching your diet and exercising should come into the picture because beliefs have to be backed up with action. On the other hand, you can exercise and diet till the cows come home but if you are not willing to even suspend the belief that you are big and oversized, you will find it very difficult to take off that weight!

Step Four

Meditation for Painful and Deep-Seated Emotions

(Taking Tea With Demons)

When you feel overwhelmed with life, it can be difficult to meditate. This is because you are trying so hard not to feel your feelings, that instead you shut down, unable to cry, breathing very shallowly. It is at times like this when we need to slow down and take a deep breath, but it's as if we have implanted a shunt in our throats.

The following technique, which I call Taking Tea With Demons (TTWD) can really help you to break through the dam of resistance that is holding you so rigidly.

What we do is we invite those feelings in, which I know is contradictory to what our natural impulse might be. In our society we have been taught to ignore our feelings and we have plenty of distractions from substances to television to help us do that. However, in the long run, the feelings reemerge because we haven't dealt with them.

What you will delightfully discover is that feelings are just feelings and they can change just like the weather does, from stormy to sunny, but they won't budge if you refuse to open the gate and let the dogs out.

1. Start by finding a comfortable place where you can remove yourself from the everyday distractions of your life. You can sit or lie down, it is up to you.

2. Use TGM to bring your attention to your breath.

3. Take a long, deep inhale and as you do think "Come on in, all of you deeply painful feelings, come right on in," and breathe deeply, allowing yourself to be open to whatever comes up.

4. On the exhale think, "I survived that, I am okay, I am stronger than my feelings," and let out a sigh of relief.

5. Repeat this over and over for a number of times. Each time you inhale, pull the feelings up and into you all the while thinking, "Come on in." If tears come, then tears come. They are probably needed. On the exhale, let out a sigh of relief, if you like, thinking, "Phew, I'm still here. I am stronger than my feelings."

Imagine what would happen if the sky held back its storms. The humidity would never break. It's a bit like that!

Expanding on Deep Seated Emotions

This meditation was inspired by the ancient Buddhist meditation practice of Tonglen, which I learned in a workshop taught by Buddhist monk and meditation teacher Pema Chödrön.

When I first learned how it worked, I was not drawn to it. It's a very compassionate practice in which you breathe in the pain of the world and send out a blessing on the exhale. Being mostly concerned with self-healing, I didn't think I could welcome in the world's pain, so I did not delve into the practice of Tonglen.

However, a year or so after my son Danny passed in July of 2008, from an overdose, I found myself feeling numb. I felt a dull sense of despair and guilt that I couldn't seem to throw off my shoulders. It just kept sticking around.

I had gone through some of the known stages of grief, from denial to sorrow to anger, but this was something different. It was as if I were in a trance state, one that didn't allow for any feelings to come through, neither pain nor joy. Instead I felt a dull ache just under the surface.

I didn't know how to move from this state of mind. Then I remembered what I had learned from Stephen Levine about coping with pain. Stephen had said that in order to end pain you had to go into it, that you could not heal it by running away from it, and that you simply had to let it pass through you. I pondered; how do I go into it and how do I let it pass through me?

Then I remembered the concept of Tonglen and thought that I might try to use it in this case by drawing into myself the thoughts, feelings and emotions that were lurking just under the surface of my awareness and gnawing away at my peace of mind and vitality.

And so I started drawing those feelings into me and what I found was that the fears I held about the feelings were groundless because they were just my feelings, and not me! Every time I relaxed on the exhale, I realized that I didn't have to be afraid of my own feelings. What I also discovered, which was the best part, was that by facing the feelings I was diffusing their power over me.

Sometimes, because I found it difficult to approach that first initial inhale of my heavy feelings, I would turn it into kind of a challenge game by thinking, (and sometimes in rather crude terms, even using curse words at times): "Come on you _____ you have nothing over me." I'll leave it to you to fill in the blanks, but for me it worked to take an aggressive approach in addressing my feelings rather than a meek one. In the end, the dam broke and I was able to breathe again more freely.

Once more I return you to the analogy of the weather. The sky would never hold back its storms and if it tried to, we would have nothing but endless humidity.

Chapter Ten

When a Philosophy Becomes the Truth
Common Sense Spirituality
The Empty Boat Theory

We all want something to believe in that can help us to feel safe or, at the very least, sane. That was certainly the case for me when I discovered The Seth Material, which explains why I was so drawn to the concepts. Nothing comforted me more than the idea that all I had to do was get my beliefs in order and I'd never have to worry about falling ill ever again. I could simply believe in my good health and completely forget about doctors altogether!

Because this idea appealed to me so greatly, I tried to mold this into my new truth. I reasoned that if I created my own reality, that I simply would not create illness and therefore did not need medical doctors. As you know, I did go back to medical doctors to reconnect my bowel in 1984, but beyond the medication I needed to regulate my bowel, I had convinced myself that I had no need for western medicine. Without realizing it, I had swung from one end of the spectrum to the other: from trusting only traditional medical science to trusting only spiritual healing. My life, however, has never allowed me to sit too comfortably in any one camp for too long.

Jerry and I entered 1989 with a mixture of challenges on our plate. Our finances were heavily invested in the real estate market, which was making a rapid decline, and taking with it our equity and net worth. Jerry worked desperately to save our business, but as we moved further into 1989, it became clear that our situation could not be reversed and this realization naturally brought a lot of stress into our home. We had two little boys now, Danny three and Aaron seven years old. The two of them together were wild and turned what had once been my beloved

Greenwich Village, into a nightmare of cars and taxi cabs racing down Seventh Avenue, forcing me to run after Danny and Aaron yelling, "Hold my hand!"

Worst of all for me, however, was that I began to experience pain in my bowel for the first time in years. At the same time I was doing promotion for the original version of this book, so you can imagine how stressed out I was feeling and although it was a thrill to see Healing from the Inside Out in bookstores, I felt like a hypocrite. Here I was the healing teacher, talking about creating my own reality and I had problems all over my life.

Up until then, it had been easy to believe that I was creating a great reality because the events of my life had unfurled like a fairy tale: the healing, the marriage, the children, the reconnection, the financial success. Similarly, it was easy to fool myself into thinking that I understood what real self-love meant, when all the little bits and pieces of my reality were falling into place. But now, amidst turmoil that I was not happy about, I found myself loaded with judgment and shame, especially around the health issue.

I was anything but kind to myself. When pain occurred I became angry at myself and mentally criticized myself for having pain again. When I most needed my own compassion, there was none to be had. Because I believed that as a healer I *should* be able to take away the pain, I refused to see a doctor and therefore lived with pain periodically for over a year. It was only after I was forced into the hospital with a serious bowel obstruction that I admitted that I needed medical attention.

Dr. Present took one look at me, my eyes sunken in my face, and asked, "Why did you wait so long before coming for help?" And I had to sit with that one. Why did I wait? Why couldn't I have come forward? Why did I feel so ashamed of the pain?

These questions plagued me. And then sitting there wide awake, as a huge male resident shoved a tube back down my nose saying, "Swallow, swallow, swallow," a scene way too reminiscent of days that I had thought could never come again, I realized that the only thing that mattered was being out of pain. I knew that I had a lot of sorting out to do. I wanted to understand the reasons by which I had dug such a huge hole for myself. I realized now that I had to stop being mad at myself for without my own compassion, there would be no room for any healing to take place. I would first have to start by forgiving myself for what I saw as my great failure: a recurrence in whatever shape or form, of the Crohn's Disease. Then I would have to open my mind up to whatever kind of help I needed whether it was spiritual or medical. Eventually I would sort out all the rest.

It was within hours of my checking into the hospital that the blockage began to break up and the pain to lessen. The physical crisis was over; however, a Pandora's box of sorts had been opened and now there were parts and pieces of my life strewn all over the floor. What to pick up, how to reorganize? I felt confused about what had happened.

I realized that even though it was brief in duration, the time that I spent feeling vulnerable and out of control had jolted me awake! I certainly didn't think of myself as fanatical or even limited in the way that I lived my life, but I knew now that this episode pointed out a major imbalance in my thinking. By taking a philosophy and trying to turn it into the truth, I became fanatical about it. Not only did I feel guilt and shame over losing my health, but I felt compelled to handle regaining it by myself, using my own methods. I assured myself that there was only one true way to achieve this, which involved working with the contents of my mind and my beliefs. I would definitely not stoop so low as to pursue any medical treatment, and because I was so very invested in upholding this "truth," it was easier to let myself suffer. Now I began to wonder what was more important to me: my image of myself, or my actual self. And then, as I sat there, trying to understand, I remembered some of Seth's words, spoken to the class on September 18, 1973.

"There is no one truth. So I cannot give you truth, and any man or ghost or spirit who offers it to you in a pill or a potion or an idea, run from him. For when he says, 'This is truth,' he is saying that everything else is not truth, and he is limiting your vision and your reality and structuring your trip."

I began to realize that I had done just that very thing. I had structured my life around a philosophy and I could not see past my own limited vision. Jerry was appalled at my refusal to see a doctor, because it was obvious to him that I needed help, but in keeping with my new "truth" to me, becoming ill again was the ultimate failure and seeking medical help was proof positive of that!

Common Sense Spirituality

I now aspire to what I refer to as common sense spirituality. Based on all I've been through, I think it's important. We aren't just spirit beings. We are not just physical bodies. We are both. While I believe that spirit infuses the body, it is not the only component here. Until we fly with wings and no longer walk with our two feet on the ground, we had better remember to stay grounded. I now believe in taking what I think of as the middle road, a path that is open to receiving both help and knowledge from a myriad of sources, mixing the modalities and finding out what works best for me. Sometimes it's going to be a western medicine, sometimes what is called for is meditation for stress reduction. When you take the middle road you can explore options on either side of the road. You don't have to pick a side.

In my case, for example, I have put together what I think of as my own personal healing prescription and it incorporates modalities from western medicine to spiritual healing and everything in between. In this way I am able to address all of my physical issues. I still test positive for the Hepatitis C Virus, I still have Crohn's Disease and I still live with a pretty huge colon deficiency. Without taking the allopathic medicine that my doctors prescribe to constipate my colon, I would never leave the bathroom! At the same time I drink alkaline water, known as "Kangen Water" which has taken the wind out of the mighty sails of Crohn's Disease. I still work with meditation everyday for many reasons, but, of course, to maintain the awareness that I am not my thoughts and to work with the healing energy.

When you travel the middle road you realize that one modality is not better than another and that they work best together. When you're not sure what to do, always remember your common sense. I look at it this way: If something crosses my desk that I am told is very helpful for one of my medical conditions, be it herbal, homeopathic or allopathic, I first investigate it to see if there are any downsides to consider. If I believe that it can't hurt me, I try it. If it helps me, I stay with it, adding it to my personal healing prescription (PHP). If it doesn't seem to help, I drop it. Now I have a whole package of goodies in my PHP basket, and I'm happy to report that I've just turned 65 and it's hard for me to believe that I was ever as sick as I was at 19!

When you take a philosophy, any philosophy and decide that it is capital letter TRUTH, you tend to organize your life in accordance with that truth. Back in the Seth classes people would debate the implications of buying health insurance, which they were sure meant that you were betting on your own poor health. Locking your front door was now a sign that you believed you were in danger of being robbed and going to the doctor was, well in Jane's own words to me, "Just looking for trouble. " It's easy to lose sight of your own common sense when a philosophy becomes the truth, however, as stated before, my life experience always intervened to wake me up and make me examine my perspective. Here's another example of that: In 1990, when Danny was in kindergarten, his teacher had a mastectomy. Naturally, all the moms were talking about mammograms and, of course, I was the oldest mother in the group, but the only one who had not had a mammogram. That evening I had a telephone conversation with a friend and explained my reasons for not having mammograms. Little did I know that my ten year old son Aaron was standing in the doorway listening in. When I hung up the phone he approached me. "Mommy," he said, "Do you know for a fact that you would not create Cancer?" he asked. "Well, no, I guess I don't know it for a fact," I answered. "So then, you'd find out about it when it was too late to do anything about it and that's the way you take care of us?" "From the mouth of babes," I thought and immediately knew that I would have to start facing those dreaded mammograms.

An interesting footnote to this story is that when I finally had my first mammogram, it didn't go smoothly. Although I have small breasts, apparently they are very dense and loaded with calcifications and other things that are normal, but hard to differentiate from cancer. Instead of being told, "Everything's fine, you can get dressed," I was informed that the doctor wanted to take some additional x rays. He wanted the x rays to be enlarged and he wanted to do a sonogram as well. Needless to say, I was pretty upset and as I stood there, sweating profusely onto the mammogram machine, a voice in my head said, "It's not that you were above having mammograms girl, it's that you weren't up to it!"

That revelation hit me like a ton of bricks! I clearly saw that because of my insurmountable fear of illness, I had wrapped the Seth concepts around me like a comfort blanket and decided to simply play ostrich, which I did successfully, until Aaron brought me face to face with my lack of common sense. Did I think that because I had adopted the Seth philosophy that I was immune to Cancer? Did these concepts provide me with such a special knowledge that I was lifted above the human condition?

Sometime after this realization I was invited to speak at a Seth Conference in Connecticut. I decided to share the above story, which probably was a mistake because, as I used to say, "If the audience had a basket of tomatoes, my face would have been dripping red!" Apparently, I had upset the applecart. I was informed that the following morning there was much negative talk about my presentation with one woman complaining that she had finally gotten to the point where she felt enough trust to forgo mammograms and that I was rocking her boat, which brings me back to the concept of the middle road. Why does it have to be either or? When you decide to take the middle road you can believe in your good health and still purchase health insurance. You can lock your doors while maintaining the belief that you are safe, and you can believe that you will remain well and still have mammograms. Even though the quantum physicists are proving the role of consciousness in the outcome of events, we still have the right to hedge our bets, don't we? The last time I checked, I still walked with two feet on the ground!

The Empty Boat Theory

When a philosophy becomes the truth, it is easy to limit your way of thinking to remain in sync with that philosophy. If you believe that you have the truth, it is easy to close off to other ways of thinking, especially if they pose a threat to your way of thinking.

Without necessarily being aware of it, you have built a fortress around yourself, locking out other possibilities. Using the analogy of a boat, it's as if you fill your boat completely with everything that you think you will need, leaving no additional space for anything but yourself. You set off in your fully equipped boat, to travel the seas of your life. It sounds like you've got it covered, however, there is one problem: when you come across a new artifact or a new concept, there is no room on-board your boat to take anything new on. Your boat is so full, that it is a prison in its own way.

It's important to keep some empty space in your boat for what has yet to present itself. If you regard the philosophies that you live your life by as hypotheses rather than as truths, you are in a much better position to expand your understanding. Leave some room in your boat for curiosity and wonder.

Chapter Eleven

What Is This Thing Called Enlightenment?

To Get a Grip, Loosen Your Grasp

Ever since the 60's there's been a lot of tossing around of the term "enlightenment." I've never understood what it means. It's always brought to mind a vague sense of being above and beyond ordinary consciousness, a place of total peace and harmony, a state of mind so elevated that you could almost walk on water. Aside from the fact that after years of trying to reach enlightenment, I realized that it was not something I was likely to achieve, in time I came to see it as an unrealistic state for anyone human to achieve, at least, in today's world.

So I wondered, what was the point to all of this meditation and affirmation if I wasn't going to become enlightened anyway, and then it occurred to me that although I didn't know what it meant to be enlightened, I certainly understood what it meant to lighten-up and maybe that was all I needed to do: to lighten-up, to not take things so seriously, to not take myself so seriously.

It seems to me that since I was a little girl, I always gripped life so tightly. I still have a good sized callous on the middle finger of my right hand where I gripped my pencil in school. As if holding on tightly would make me safe, I braced myself against my fears, not understanding that the brace was strangling me.

It's very common to brace ourselves, to feel that in order to get a grasp, we need to grab on and hold tightly. Many of us struggle to keep solid ground under our feet but here's the paradox: There is no solid ground! Everything changes. Nothing stays the same. How can we attain solid ground when everything is always shifting and changing?

The truth is, we can't. Ultimately all we can do is lighten our grip on the rope of life and allow life to flow through our fingers, because I assure you, the tighter you grip that rope, the more painful the rope burns will be. Now that's just common sense, however, old habits die hard and resisting what we don't like has become a way of life. So, what can we do?

I read a book in 1970 when I was 19 years old titled "The Handbook to Higher Consciousness" by Ken Keyes. I thought back then that Keyes was on to something. I have traveled many paths and tried out many ideologies since then, and I still think Keyes is on to something. Keyes talked about what he called "Upgrading our addictions to preferences, " and I see wisdom in these words, especially when it comes to the concept of attachment.

We all have attachments. We all want things to go our way. Sometimes they do. Sometimes they really don't. It may sound like a small thing, but it changes a lot when you can step back and say, "I would have loved it, but I don't have to have it." It doesn't mean that you are not disappointed, it doesn't mean that you won't cry, but it does take some of the charge out of your experience, because you are loosening your grasp on that rope.

A book was published in 2002 by Byron Katie with the title "Loving What Is." I had a hard time with that title because I wouldn't ask anyone to love Cancer, or to love attending their own child's funeral. But I understand the wisdom of coming to terms with what is and finding a way to cope, possibly even thrive.

Personally, I hate the fact that my son passed from an overdose at age 22. There's not one silver lining or lesson to be learned that will get me to say, that where Danny is concerned, I love what is. But I will say that I have accepted what is and that I am making the best of it, finding ways to maintain a different kind of relationship with Danny which is very joyous for me. Now there are quite a few people I have worked with who say that they want their child back in their body as he or she was and that if they can't have that, then they don't want anything at all, and so they get nothing at all.

Of course it's my preference that Danny be alive in his body today, but since that cannot be, upgrading my addiction to a preference saves me. It also helps Dan who has expressed gratitude through medium Glenn Dove for the fact that we (myself and my husband) are allowing him to be there without putting guilt on him. It helps everyone around you, but no one more than yourself, when you decide to do this.

Interestingly, when we get worked up, there is a biological reaction that takes place that actually makes it much more difficult for us to work out viable solutions. Stem cell biologist Bruce Lipton explains that when we get excited, biologically our bodies react by directing our blood away from our brains and into our extremities. Because, we are still mammals, instinctively our bodies go into "fight or flight response." "So, you know what happens people?" Bruce goes on to say, "You get stupider!" And so, if we lose our cool when we need to focus and think, we are more like chickens with our heads cut off! We don't get a grip, we get chaos!

I'll admit that much of this is easier said than done. But you practice with the little challenges in your life as they come up, and in time, you are able to loosen your grasp even around bigger things. I highly recommend that you work with this one, because no matter how positively you think or how healthily you eat, you just never know what's coming around the bend.

Chapter Twelve

Self Love ... Becoming Your Own Best Ally
Forget Perfection, Embrace Your Individuality

Your self-love is, in my opinion, the single most important ingredient necessary for your wellness and happiness. Yourdictionary.com defines self-love as the belief you hold that you are a valuable and worthy person. I believe, without that, we feel lost in a world where we don't matter!

We all need to know that we matter. Although, we may never be famous in the eyes of the world, we all need to know that each of our lives have meaning.

Unfortunately, we are not taught anything about this in our schools. We accumulate a lot of facts about the outside world, but our inner feelings are overlooked. They are not brought out into the open, examined and evaluated as a science question would be. They are simply ignored. No wonder so many people suffer from depression!

I'm sure that most of our parents and caretakers did the best that they could raising us, but since we also learn nothing about child raising in school, most of us enter this incredibly important job not having a clue what to do. Growing up in the 50's parents tended to be stricter and to criticize their children, believing that in this way they would make their children better. Nothing could be further from the truth! Today you hear more talk about parents being overindulgent, parents who converse with their children with questions such as: "Do you want white milk or do you want chocolate milk? Do you want to eat or do you want to play?" letting, as Jerry (my husband) puts it, the inmates run the asylum. Either way, the point I'm trying to make is that when it comes to this all- important job of raising a human being, most of us shoot from the hip and inevitably, we make mistakes. Not realizing how vulnerable and open the minds of small children are, parents can mobilize their children to download negative assumptions and beliefs that will shape their perceptions for the rest of their lives. Whether they believe that they are good, whether they believe that they have value, much of this will begin to take form very early.

We all know that there are many who suffered terrible abuses from their caretakers, and for them, the climb out of that rabbit hole is arduous. Many of us don't come near that kind of childhood trauma and yet, still feel unworthy. Wherever you are on that totem pole, your happiness is waiting for you to climb up and out of the rabbit hole and into the light of self-love.

No greater pain exists than the inability or unwillingness to love and approve of yourself, but it is up to you to investigate your own perspective and discover how you see yourself, how you talk to yourself and ultimately, how you treat yourself.

As you work with the healing program, much of this will be revealed to you. When you jot down the thoughts and ideas that you are habitually focusing on, you will see many of the seeds of your suffering. That is the first step, because until you can see something, you are blind to its existence in your life. It may be a painful, limiting belief that you are struggling with, but you simply assume that it's a fact of life and it remains unchallenged.

In Woody Allen's movie Annie Hall, the character played by Woody, (Alvy Singer) explains to Annie, (played by Diane Keaton) his view of life. He explains that in his opinion, people fit into one of two categories, the horrible or the miserable. He goes on to explain that the horrible refers to people with crippling illnesses, deformities, just terrible life situations, and the miserable refers to everybody else. Now this was meant to be a joke, but there is a lot of truth in it. We can't expect people born into extreme poverty, war conditions, or illnesses of a physical or mental nature not to suffer, but even people whose cups runneth over with blessings, can be miserable a good deal of the time. This should not be.

We live in a world in which way too many people are unhappy and can't seem to find any lasting satisfaction. Sure, on television and billboards everyone's got that big white teethed smile, but that's all acting, selling us a persona. God only knows what's beneath that smile that you don't see.

Becoming Your Own Best Ally

Wouldn't it be nice if, when things went wrong, the voice in your head was loving and supportive rather than angry and judgmental?

Many find that when things go wrong, they have a harsh critic inside their head who only makes matters worse. Years ago, when I began to clearly hear the critic in my head I was understandably upset and began to question myself: "Would I talk that way to my best friend, or my child or my mate?" I realized I would not.

I remember a day when I was first living in Manhattan. I had just started teaching Seth classes and accidentally jammed the copy machine at my husband's office while making transcripts of the class material for the students. Well, I felt so badly, you would have thought that I had shot someone! I returned to my neighborhood and immediately headed out to the local copy store, holding back tears the entire time. I felt so guilty and then, while waiting in the store I glanced down at the class material in my hand, which was on the subject of trusting our basic goodness. I realized that I was beating myself up over a little mistake.

All of a sudden, it didn't seem like such a big deal. I realized that underlying my reaction to this event was my belief in my basic unworthiness. I thought to myself, "I had better do something about this," and then an idea came to my mind. As I walked home from the copy store I began to recite the following affirmation to myself:

On the inhale I mentally said:
My being is good
On the exhale:
My body is good
Again on the inhale:
My life is good
Again on the exhale:
And I am good

I repeated this over and over and I started to feel better. "Yeah," I thought, "I'm a good person and good people can make mistakes." Now that particular affirmation was tailor-made to meet my needs, however, the beauty of this is that once you see your own areas of need, you can construct the affirmations you need.

As I became more involved in watching my thoughts, I saw that I was more critical of myself than I was supportive. I decided that when situations came up that pushed my buttons I would watch my reactions and ask myself three questions: "If this was my best friend, would I talk to her like this? If this was my only child, would I admonish him like that? If this was my mate who I cared for, would I treat him like this?" I knew that in each case, I would be kinder.

I began to see that all of this had to change in order for me to become a happier, more confident person. By virtue of my reaction to the "copy machine event", I knew that I had to start with changing how I saw myself. If my self-worth hadn't been in question, the event would have amounted to nothing more than a simple mistake and I could have let it pass over. But, instead, because underneath I really didn't feel good about myself, I blew the whole thing way out of proportion and beat myself up.

That was the beginning of my work on becoming my own best ally. I worked with the "discovery" and "reprogramming" end of things for years and I can tell you, without any hesitation that I am a far cry from the girl I once was. I am so much easier on myself and so much less afraid. Am I fearless? Hell no. Do I still at times put myself down? Sure. But, the difference between the 20 year old Sheri, and Sheri at 65 is like night and day!

I am very grateful to any teacher, book or philosophy that has guided me in the direction of loving and trusting myself, however, I'm also grateful to myself for doing the work, because that's the thing, you have to do the work. It's well worth the effort though, because only you can set yourself free!

As I said, some beliefs can change easily, just by seeing that they are not necessarily facts of reality, but other beliefs will need you to look them in the eye and reject them. But again, you are not your thoughts or your beliefs. You are the awareness in which they exist and you can get into the nuts and bolts of your mind and discard whatever you find in there that is self-destructive.

Now, there are those who will tell you that by working with your beliefs you can achieve much more than I am talking about. They say that by changing your beliefs you can heal your body, become rich, and in general create your reality as you want it to be. This idea comes not only from the "Seth" material but it is the crux of The Laws of Attraction, The Secret, the Abraham Hicks books and I'm sure many other teachings. Quantum physics points as well to the idea that expectations affect outcome.

However, I want to clearly state here that I am not writing about that. I am not talking about creating physical reality. I am talking about a psychological state in which you feel good about yourself, despite all those things that you see as your imperfections and that you are kind to yourself whether your life is going well or not.

When I had the recurrence of Crohn's Disease, I was in no condition to help myself. I was so hung up on the idea that I was responsible for the disease, that I couldn't be responsible to the disease or to myself. I was the furthest thing from an ally to myself and this is what I'm talking about because this shouldn't be. I came to realize that if it was easy to create the reality of our choice, no one would have cancer and everyone would be rich! I trust that along with what we want and believe, there are other factors that must come into play. I can list many of the well-known theories from Karma to Soul Choice, but as my buddy Reverend Dr. Joyce Liechenstein is fond of saying, "What do we really know for sure?" What I know for sure is that, for me, there is still some mystery in this ball of wax we call life and before those mysteries I am indeed humbled.

I buried a son. I know what it feels like to want one thing and end up with quite the opposite. So I have a healthy respect for the unknown hand of God.

On the other hand, I do know that my thoughts and beliefs affect my perceptions, feelings and actions. It is about that, that I speak, because we can be our own best ally or our own worst enemy. I know because I've been both and I thank God that ally is winning out!

No matter what happens to you, you can learn to be as kind and supportive to yourself as a best friend, loving parent or caring mate would. This to me is the crux of healing. If you are unable to cure your cancer, you can still love yourself, if you're never going to be rich, you can still respect yourself and if fame isn't in the cards for you, understand that you can still affect the world around you.

This life on earth has built-in challenges. Just living with the fear of losing a child could drive a human mother half mad. But this is the life we are living on earth at this time. We can't change that. What we can change is how we go through the days of our lives. Whether we befriend or defriend ourselves is in our hands alone.

Forget About Perfection

One of the reasons we are so hard on ourselves is because we all measure ourselves against some ideal of perfection, which is a losing battle. As Seth used to say, "Flesh and blood has many dimensions. Perfection is not one of them," and we all know, from our own experience that this is true.

The reason I say to forget about perfection altogether is because perfection suggests a state of being in which something is finished, complete, and beyond improvement; for example, a statue. Nothing that is living and growing can ever be finished. Wherever I am today, I can learn more tomorrow, see another picture, take something new into my boat, throw something that doesn't work out. The very nature of what I am isn't even in the ballpark of "finished", and I believe that who I am will continue to grow even after this physical life ends. If perfection means what I think it does, it's an impossibility for any of us to achieve, and therefore shouldn't even be one of our goals.

When I was younger I would say, "I am going to create the best reality and then I'll be happy." Now I say only, "Whatever happens, I'll show up and I'll do my best."

They say a perfectionist is someone who can't realize perfection. Sometimes we have perfectly fine mates, nice kids, good friends, but they too are imperfect and sometimes let us down. We can become disappointed in them and push back and, of course, we run the same kind of routine with ourselves.

I don't remember exactly when this was, but at some point it came to me to simply decide that I was a good enough wife and a good enough mother. I felt a huge relief when I did this and so I decided to spread that perspective outward and allow my husband to be a good enough mate and then for my children to be good enough, my friends and on and on from there. You know what happened? My world became a friendlier place. Starting with becoming my own ally allowed me to ease up on the others in my life.

Nobody's perfect and everybody has challenges of one kind or another. Not denying any of that, I still believe that our internal happiness has a lot to do with our outlook. That's what I'm talking about.

Embrace Your Individuality

I am fond of Seth's word for God which is "All-that-is" because it's inclusive of everything in the universe, including each one of us. We are all a part of this gestalt of energy, a tiny but significant part of All-that-is and so when we deny ourselves love we deny love to God as well, for we are a part of God as a wave is a part of the ocean. We rise up out of it, but we are not separate from it. We are a part of it while at the same time we are ourselves, unique and individual.

Instead of comparing ourselves to others, or to some ideal of the perfect self, we need to accept ourselves as good enough. That's all that it takes. You don't have to be better than and you don't have to be the best. You just have to be you. If you have a loud voice, then have a loud voice! If you're really short, then be really short. Certainly, in areas that cannot be changed, let whatever you are be good enough.

When you honor your individuality and accept yourself for who you are, it is known throughout your cells. It is the kindest, most healing thing you can do for yourself.

When I came to see that I was not my thoughts, or my beliefs, but the being in which all those thoughts existed, I became less patient with self-destructive ways of thinking. I realized that although I was not my thoughts, that they certainly could hurt me and that it was up to me to take the bull by the horns and simply declare: "I am Sheri Perl. I am who I am and what I am is good. I'm not perfect, but I'm good enough and I'm simply not going to listen to anymore commentary." Sometimes, I can just leave the whole kit and caboodle in the dust.

Chapter Thirteen

Eternity is Real/Death is a Myth

Goosing Yourself with Impermanence
Paying Something Forward

If I had to pick, I would say that the most important thing I learned from Harry Edwards is that there is indeed a realm of spirit that we all enter into when we die, a realm where we go on being ourselves, only leaving behind our physical bodies.

I learned this from my healing experience. Today countless numbers of people are coming to the same conclusion, that there is a realm of spirit, as a result of having Near Death Experiences. NDE's (near death experiences) take place when a person is declared clinically dead and is then revived. During that time of clinical death, their spirits leave their bodies and visit that realm of spirit, which most NDEers call Heaven because they are so overwhelmed by the beauty and majesty of what they have seen and experienced there.

When one person says that they see white light and feel caressed by unconditional love, it is easy to dismiss it as a hallucination, however, when thousands of people report the same or similar experiences, it points to the validity of their claims. If you are interested in learning more about these phenomenal accounts, I would recommend reading "Life After Life" by Dr. Raymond Moody, who has spent years researching and recording these experiences, each one more compelling than the next.

Something that is very universal is the psychological change that takes place in individuals who have had an NDE experience, or any experience, that opened their eyes to the presence of the spirit realm. Once they came to know that life doesn't end here on earth, everything changed.

So very significant is the loss of the fear and trepidation that has surrounded death since man roamed the earth. From the cavemen to the Millennials, the idea of annihilation has never sat comfortably with any of us. We just can't imagine not being, and that may very well be because such a state doesn't exist. There is no end or demise to what we are and although we shed our physical bodies at death, our essence, that which looks out from behind our physical eyes, continues on in the realm of spirit.

Eben Alexander MD wrote a wonderful book that I love and highly recommend entitled *Proof of Heaven - A Neurosurgeon's Journey Into the Afterlife*. In the book Eben describes his life-changing NDE that took place while he was in a week-long coma, brought on by a case of Meningitis, so severe, that he was declared brain dead by his physicians. With no brain activity whatsoever, there is no way that Eben's experience could have been the product of hallucinations generated by his cerebral cortex.

After Eben recovered and his consciousness reawakened in his body, he was able to describe his experience in detail, although he says words cannot do justice to an experience so illuminating and gratifying. Although I imagine he still practices neurosurgery, much of his time is spent writing, lecturing and spreading the good news that eternity is real and that death is a myth. He feels it is important for people to know that beyond their physical lives there is a realm of spirit, and that it is beautiful and loving beyond our wildest dreams.

When you come to understand that you are not merely the product of some accidental big bang in the sky and that there is a bigger picture in which you have your place, a greater sense of peace can begin to grow in you. The following quote is from Eben's second book, *The Map of Heaven*; "Heaven makes us human. We forget it at our peril. Without knowledge of the larger geography of where we came from and where we are going again when our physical bodies die, we are lost." Eben Alexander MD. I know I was. Growing up as I did with no concept of spirit or an afterlife, I was terrified. That's why I suggest that you investigate spirituality. Whether you meditate, read, listen to Cd's, go to seminars or just open your mind, exploring spirituality will add a dimension to your life that will help you.

Goosing Yourself With Impermanence

I personally believe in what I call goosing myself with impermanence. This means reminding myself on a daily basis that I am going to die. It may sound morbid but it's definitely not. It's a reminder.

As much as we all think we know this, I am always amazed at how we take things for granted. It's as if we have this built-in denial mechanism that insulates us, so that even though we know that our death and the death of all physical things is a fact, we don't live that way. We live as if we have forever to love the people in our lives and appreciate what we have.

Denial is built-in and we just seem to fall into it. We think that it makes life more bearable, however, it blurs our vision. It stops us from seeing the miracles of physical life that are happening all around us.

So, sometimes I like to goose myself into awareness. Here's something that will wake you up real fast: Just imagine, if you will, that you have been informed that this is the last day of your physical life on earth. Just think of all the things that you would want to do and see and feel, just one more time. You would be overwhelmed by the amazing amount of things that you love about life.

All of a sudden things that you have taken for granted and possibly even ignored, have ultimate meaning to you.

Goosing yourself with the concept of impermanence has other benefits as well. When you take in the concept of death, a lot of pettiness falls away. You can still see the imperfections of your loved ones, but you just don't care as much. It changes your perspective and helps you to focus on what's really important. Now, this does not mean that you accept the unacceptable, nor does it suggest that you become a doormat for anyone. But it does suggest cutting the people you love some slack.

Maybe it's just some psychological trick, but knowing that your life is impermanent generates appreciation in a way that nothing else will. All of a sudden an evening out to dinner with a good friend becomes a priceless event.

I don't know why we don't ordinarily have this kind of vision, but, I assure you, if you goose yourself with your own impermanence from time to time, that will do the trick.

Paying Something Forward

They say that life is for learning. Sometimes I think, "It had better be, or we're just a bunch of masochists! I mean why would we even choose to take birth in an impermanent realm where we can lose everyone we love?

But the truth is, everything matters more, precisely because it is impermanent and rather than deny this fact, I believe we should embrace it. Embrace it and let it remind us that the time is now to love ourselves and those around us and when we are strong enough, to send that love even to those we don't know, because they are sentient beings too.

Although this is a self-help book, I don't mean for that help to be limited to the self. If you are still treading water, take care of yourself, but if you can stay afloat, pay something forward. Every creature in this world needs love and any small act of kindness promotes healing.

I leave you with that thought and the knowledge that my door is always open to you, if I can be of service.

I will end this in the words of my beloved Harry Edwards: "May all healing blessings be with you."

CPSIA information can be obtained at www.ICGtesting.com
Printed in the USA
BVOW04s1653061016

464311BV00001B/1/P

9 780984 666515